BECOMING A DYNAMIC
YOUTH
LEADER

A GUIDE FOR EQUIPPING
VOLUNTEER YOUTH WORKERS

by Larry Maxwell

Church Growth Institute

Providing Practical Tools for Growth

P.O. Box 4404, Lynchburg, VA 24502

Editor: Cindy G. Spear
Editorial and Design Assistant: Tamara Johnson
Cover Designer: Carolyn R. Phelps
Cover Illustrator: Bob Beasley

Scriptures in this text are the King James Version of
the Holy Bible unless otherwise noted.

Copyright 1993, Church Growth Institute
All Rights Reserved
First Printing, July 1993
Printed in the United States of America
ISBN #0-941005-88-7

CONTENTS

INTRODUCTION

Introduction

There is a tremendous need for dynamic youth ministry. The significant number of young people in the world (almost 25 percent of the world's population are teenagers), the unique struggles and challenges they face, and our Lord's command to "preach the Gospel to every creature" (Mark 16:15) compels every church to develop a dynamic youth ministry that reaches out to teenagers.

My first ministry position was with teens. I believed youth ministry was important and knew it could change lives. Now more than 20 years later, having worked with hundreds of youth leaders and thousands of teens, I am convinced beyond a shadow of a doubt that youth ministry is absolutely essential and that it can be very effective if proper principles of youth work are learned and applied.

Some of the most important decisions in life are made during our days as a young person. One survey of full-time Christian workers discovered that most of them surrendered for the ministry before the age of 25. Another survey found more than 85 percent of those who trusted Christ as Saviour, did so by the time they reached the age of 18. That means only 15 percent of those who trusted Christ did so after age 18.

Ministering to teenagers can be one of the most productive, life-changing ministries in which you can be involved. You can experience the joy of helping teens make the transition from childhood to adulthood. You can help lead and guide them in a positive way as they make decisions that affect them for the rest of their lives.

Would you like to make a difference in the lives of young people, one which will last for all eternity? You can if you are willing to make a commitment, a commitment to learn how to minister *effectively* to young people. No matter how small or how large your church is or how many workers you may have, when someone like you makes a commitment to learn how to minister more effectively to teens, your church can have a dynamic youth ministry.

To minister effectively to teens you must learn a few things. First you need to learn how to understand them. You must remember the world has changed drastically from the days when you were a teen. Some of the influences and issues facing teens today are totally different from what you faced.

You need to understand the elements which are essential for effective youth ministry. Some youth programs have a positive influence in the lives of their teens but could be more productive if they understood and included each of the essential elements for effective youth ministry in their program.

You need to understand the team leadership concept and learn how to put it to work in your own youth ministry. Even if you start out as the only team member, one day as you work at building your teens, your team will grow.

You must learn how to develop Christian character in the lives of your young people. Teens need to realize that God is concerned about every area of their lives, and must learn how to walk with God on a daily basis. They need help and guidance in this area – help which you can provide.

You need to learn *what* to teach and *how* to teach young people. Teaching young people is essential. It is often done too haphazardly without specific goals. Determine exactly what it is your teens need to know, then learn how to most effectively communicate that to them.

You need to know how to conduct a youth meeting. This is often the focal point of your youth ministry. The elements to include and the principles for conducting a youth meeting apply to whatever youth program you use or choose to develop.

You also need to know how to plan and carry out meaningful youth activities. All activities should have a purpose and a plan to accomplish that purpose. Offer activities which provide recreation and dating opportunities for your young people, but also plan evangelistic activities.

Another very important aspect of youth ministry is a practical and exciting Christian service program for your teens. Young people are full of energy and are capable of serving the Lord. They need to be challenged and trained to serve and given specific opportunities for service.

This book will help you understand young people and how to minister effectively to them. Applying the information in this book will help you either start a dynamic youth ministry or transform your current youth ministry into one which is dynamic and ministers to the total person.

I am grateful for the various youth workers who had an effect on my life as I was growing up and who each contributed in some way to my training in youth ministry. Those workers with AWANA, Boys Brigade, Campus Life, Word of Life and the various churches I grew up in, all had a lasting impact on my life. Without the investment of their time and lives, this book would not have been possible. I wish to thank Gordon Luff, Dennis Henderson, Dr. Frank Schmitt, Dr. Jerry Falwell and Dave Adams who each showed me the importance of doing a first class job in youth ministry. I want to thank Jack Wyrtzen, Harry Bollback and Paul Bubar who drilled into me the importance of enthusiasm and doctrinal purity in youth work. I want to thank Lou Nichols and Dan Knickerbocker who transformed my spiritual life by sharing with me practical advice on how to have consistent daily devotions. And I am especially grateful to the preacher who took the time to speak to a bunch of young people at a skating rink in Levittown, New York the night I trusted Christ as my Savior. And I look forward to seeing Don "Uncle Robbie" Robertson when I get to glory, the one who invested so many of his years reaching young people. I will never forget the night he challenged me to dedicate my life to the Lord in Christian service. May the fruit of these faithful workers produce fruit in your life and in the lives of the young people you minister to. Remember the exhortation of 2 Timothy 2:2; "And the things that thou hast heard of me among many witnesses, the same commit thou to faithful men, who shall be able to TEACH OTHERS ALSO."

CHAPTER ONE

CHAPTER ONE
Understanding Young People

You Can Be an Effective Youth Worker

The first step to having an effective ministry to teens is to learn how to understand them. You must seek to understand their age group characteristics, the influences in their lives, and the issues they face. Teenagers are at a time in their lives when they are going through a lot of changes which bring some real challenges and struggles. They need dedicated workers who will work at understanding them.

No one is born with a natural understanding of teenagers. Learning how to understand teens takes prayer, counsel, study, purposeful observation, and involvement with them. You can and must learn to understand teens if you ever want to be as effective as God wants you to be in your ministry with them.

To gain a better understanding of teens, the first thing to do is ask God for wisdom. He promised He would give you wisdom if you recognize you need it and sincerely ask Him for it (James 1:5). God made teenagers. He understands them and wants you to understand them too. Therefore, He will help you understand them if you ask Him.

Next, read books and information about teens and youth ministry. Be sure the books you read are written by those who work with or who have worked with teens. Some people who write materials about and for teens do not work with them. An arm chair knowledge about teenagers will never do.

Another great source of information about teens are those who work with them. Talk with other youth workers. Ask them questions. Learn what they know. Remember that experience can be a great teacher. Seek out people with experience.

Everyone involved in any type of ministry should compile a list of others who are effective in the same area of ministry. Call or write these counselors for advice. Don't just use one person for advice. Remember, "...in the multitude of counselors there is safety" (Prov. 11:14). Each person from whom you seek advice will have a different perspective and can offer different insights. Not all advice is good advice, but there is usually something you can glean from it which will help you.

You can learn a lot about teens by watching them. This does not mean you should sit across from their school and stare at them through your binoculars. It does mean you should take time to notice them whenever they are around you. Watch them at church, at the store or wherever you go. What do they wear? What do they do? What do they say?

Go to some places where teens go so you can observe them in their "natural setting." Go to the pizza place where they hang out or to school sports activities. Pay a visit to the school they attend. That can be a real eye opener.

One other absolutely essential way to learn more about teens is *to spend time with them*. Do things together. Go to a game or activity with them. Go to the store or for a walk with them. Talk with them. Be sure to let them do most of the talking. Remember, teens act differently with you around than when they are just with a group of friends.

Incorporate all of these information-gathering techniques into your life to learn about teens. This is something you will need to do over and over again.

Understanding the Individual

You will work with quite a variety of individuals in your youth ministry. Every teen you have contact with is important to God and should be important to you.

Each teen has a different background which helps make them the individual they are. Take time to understand the different factors which have had an affect on their lives.

You must recognize they are in a state of transition between childhood and adulthood. Try to understand the changes they are going through.

Teens are part of a group known as adolescents. Understanding the general characteristics of this age group will help you better understand individuals. Adolescents generally comprise ages 12 through 25. Early adolescents are comprised of junior high students, ages 12 to 15. These are usually in grades 7 through 9. Middle adolescents are comprised of high school students, ages 15 to 18. These are usually in grades 10 through 12.

Definite differences exist within each age group. For example, seventh-grade boys are not usually that interested in girls when they first enter your youth group, but by the time they reach ninth grade that interest may definitely be present. Another example is the difference between the reasoning powers of a tenth-grader and a twelfth-grader. They are often very significant.

Identify the differences between those in the group you work with. Then identify the similarities between the groups and capitalize on them.

If you have a smaller church you may have both junior and senior high teens together for your youth ministry. You can have an effective ministry with all your teens together but it takes a lot of work. It is very important to identify the differences and similarities between them.

Some churches, who do not have to, keep all their teens together and think they have a very good teen ministry. They often fail to realize they have a lot more younger teens than older teens due to the fact that the older ones do not like being with the younger ones because of the differences between them. If you must have all your teens together, you can work around this with creative planning and by involving your older teens as leaders. A good aim would be to train some other leaders so you could divide your youth ministry into separate junior and senior high groups. You could still do some activities or functions with both groups together from time to time.

Characteristics of the Junior High Student
Ages 12 to 15 (Grades 7 through 9)

This is a time of significant change. Physically vast hormonal development is taking place. The girls who enter this group are physically women and capable of reproduction by the time they leave. The change in the boys shows in their height. Some may grow as much as six to twelve inches during these three grades.

The early teen years are filled with enthusiasm and energy. These teens love activity. They do not want to be spectators, they want to be participants. They often do not realize the need for rest, though they need it because of the rapid physical development they are experiencing.

Those physical changes can bring along some real problems, both physically and emotionally as they try to cope with them. The boys may seem clumsy, tripping and spilling things all the time, because their limbs are growing more rapidly than they realize. Acne and oily complexion plague many in this age group. Advertisers love to overemphasize these changes and make them sound horrible.

The physical changes have an effect socially as individuals want to become part of the group. To fit in with a group of friends, a junior high student may adopt unusual fads or seek to have the most current fashions. Some use this to compensate for their own lack of self-acceptance which they make up for with group acceptance.

Remember how important friendships are to this age group and how they can have a long-lasting affect on the lives of your teens. Proverbs 13:20 warns us about the influence of friends, "He that walketh with wise men shall be wise: but a companion of fools shall be destroyed."

The mental abilities of this group develops almost as fast as their physical growth. They can reason more than they did when they were younger. They are ready not only for the "who?" "what?" "when?" and "where?" but also for the "why?" In fact, they are extremely "why" conscious. You must remember they do not have the ability to evaluate and weigh all the factors regarding an issue. They tend to make conclusions and decisions based more on feeling than reason.

Very few in this age group can handle abstract reasoning. They can look at the facts, and make deductions based on the facts, but they cannot understand abstract truths such as eternity and its implications, though they can accept them as truths.

When teaching this age group it is important to understand their attention span. A general rule of thumb regarding attention span is to figure one minute of attention span per year of physical growth. Thus a 14-year-old would have about a 14-minute attention span. If you cause them to sit and pay attention to one thing for more than 14 minutes you will begin to lose them. Attention span can be regained by shifting attention with participation, illustrations, and activity.

Characteristics of the High School Student
Ages 15 to 18 (Grades 10 through 12)

The physical changes in the high school student continue, but often not as rapidly as they did in the junior high student. Some boys will experience a growth spurt just as they enter high school but the rate of growth decreases by the time they are ready to leave this group.

Students in this age group will often have an adult body. Some of them will even be taller than their parents. This can be confusing for both the teen and the adult when they fail to recognize that although the teen may have an adult body, he or she is not an adult.

This group should not be called young adults, because they are not. Young adults is a better designation for those ages 18 to 25. The high-school-age adolescent may have an adult body does not have an adult mind. That does not mean they cannot think, nor does it mean they are not as smart as adults. Some of them are smarter than some adults. What they lack is the developed ability for abstract reasoning and experience which is part of the educational and maturity process.

This group does not like to be referred to as "boys and girls" or as "young people." They like to think of themselves as closer to adults, though definitely distinct.

The completion of their physical development has emotional and social consequences. Attraction to the opposite sex becomes very real. This group can experience true love, though infatuation and physical desire are often mistaken for love.

Their feelings are intense and they will try to control them. The desire for being with the opposite sex is a strong force to be reckoned with. If they allow it to control their lives they will be willing to forsake their group to be with the one they like. They may even abandon their own standards and principles for physical satisfaction.

Though physical desires and appetites exercise a strong influence on this age group, they can learn to control them as they consider the consequences of their actions. A high-school-aged teen with direction and purpose in life is more likely to exercise self-control and personal discipline than one without such goals.

This group begins to determine a direction and purpose in their lives. They know they must consider the future and begin to develop personal convictions to guide them through it. They want to know why they should believe or accept something. They want something relevant.

As teens move through the high school years they begin to become more of an individual and are more willing to stand apart from the group. Some develop leadership qualities while others remain followers.

Understanding the Influences on Young People

Understanding the various influences teens face is very important for youth workers – and parents. Some of these influences have a tremendous pull on their lives and all of them have a significant impact on their lives.

1. Home

One of the primary influences on teens is their home life. Parents, siblings, and extended family all have an influence on teens. Sometimes that influence is good, sometimes it is not. The home life can either reinforce or contradict what you are trying to accomplish.

Many teens come from broken homes. With the alarming rise in divorces, more than 50 percent of all teens now live in homes with only one natural parent.

Many teens crave the love of an absent father or mother. They may look for that love in a sympathy relationship with another teen or through a youth leader. That is dangerous. There is a lot of immorality between teens, and between youth leaders and teens, who do not recognize this problem.

Families who follow God's principles for the family and who follow biblical discipline can have a tremendously positive influence on their teens.

In many families biblical principles are foreign ideas. Their lifestyles, habits, and goals will often yield a negative influence. Most will not follow biblical discipline. Teens who have not experienced biblical discipline as a child will have a hard time with self-discipline as they grow older.

2. School

Next to the family, the school a teen attends has the greatest influence on his or her life. Just what type of influence school will have on teens depends on the educational philosophy of the institution.

Most schools are intent on shaping and molding lives. If they have a humanistic perspective, their influence will be diametrically opposed to biblical principles. Many good teens are corrupted by the philosophy of their teachers and the administration of the school (Col. 2:8).

At this time in their lives teens spend more time listening to their teachers than they do to almost anyone else. Teachers stand in a place of authority in their lives, either consciously or subconsciously. The philosophy of the teacher affects the information that is passed on and the attitude with which it is conveyed. This is implanted in the mind of the students and has a definite effect.

Other school personnel such as the office, janitorial or kitchen staff who have contact with the teens also exert an influence. Fellow students also have a tremendous influence, either negative or positive.

Remember that the average high school student is in school for at least 30 hours a week. Who else do they spend 30 of their best waking hours with each week?

3. Friends

Teens may not have a choice about what school they go to or who their teachers are or who their fellow students will be, but they can choose their friends.

You can learn a lot about someone by the friends they choose. Because teens do choose their friendships, friends can have some of the greatest influence on their lives. They will become like those they spend time with. The love of a friend is a strong bond.

4. Media

One of the most life-shaping influences teens face is directed at them by the media. Television, radio, and printed media targets the teens. The fashions and colloquialisms in the media today are the norm for tomorrow. What teens watch or listen to is imbedded in their minds and affects their attitudes, reasoning, and actions. This is often one of the most godless influences in their lives. If this is not controlled it will control them.

5. Church

The church and especially the church youth ministry should have a real and lasting impact on the lives of the teens in its community. Some churches are content to influence only those teens who attend their services or programs. Others seek to exert a positive influence on every teen in the community.

The church ministry to teens must be relevant and must be carefully planned. Of all the influences in the lives of teens, this is the one that gets the least amount of time. That time must be used wisely and purposefully.

A good youth ministry can counteract many of the negative influences a teen faces. Remember, many of the problems you see manifested in teens is because of the influences surrounding them. They can rise above those influences with your help.

Understanding the Issues Teens Face

Teens face a number of important issues of which every youth worker must be aware.

1. Self-Acceptance

As teens move from childhood to adulthood they begin to recognize themselves as more of an individual. They begin to ask such questions as, Who am I? and, Why am I here? Sometimes they wonder if God made a mistake when He made them.

Teens need to learn that God loves them and made them a beautiful person unique from everyone else, with a unique purpose for their lives (Ps. 139:13-16). They need to learn to accept God's standards for themselves instead of the world's standards. If they can learn to accept God's standards they will be able to accept themselves. If they accept the world's standards they will have trouble trying to conform to the world because they will either be too short, too tall, too fat, too thin, their hair will be too straight or too curly, their complexion too oily or too dry. The world will then try to squeeze them into a mold with its fashions, languages, and activities which are supposed to make them more acceptable.

When teens learn to stand alone with the Lord Jesus Christ and accept His standards, plan, and purpose for their lives, they can find victory in the area of self-acceptance.

2. Philosophies

Teens have to deal with a variety of philosophies held by their teachers, the media moguls, and their friends. A person's philosophy is the framework from which they make their life's decisions.

The ridiculous unscientific teaching of evolution has perpetrated a social Darwinism which is fed by humanism and atheism or by an agnostic world view. Man becomes the center of the universe and survival of the species becomes the driving force. Many teens have to deal with those who hold to this view. Those who hold this view often regard belief in God as distasteful and seek to discourage it.

For those with a recognition of a supernatural force behind the scheme of things, the New Age philosophy seeks to combine old Hinduistic teachings regarding the supernatural and self-actualization and tries to make it compatible with Christianity and other religions.

Teens need to recognize there is a Christian world view based on the Bible which provides a solid framework based on the Way, the Truth, and the Life, which alone can bring true freedom. It is the only reliable philosophy on which to build one's life.

3. Making Decisions

Every day teens are faced with the necessity of making decisions. They need to determine what the standard of truth is for their lives. They need to know the difference between what is right and wrong. They need principles to help them to know how to deal with the gray areas in life. What do they do when something is not apparently right or wrong? They need to know the importance of seeking good counsel so they can find the right answers and joy in their lives (Ps. 1:1).

4. Personal Standards

Teens may conform to outward rules, but in this rapidly changing world they need personal convictions about what to do and what not to do. They need to learn how to love God and live to His glory within their culture (Col. 3:17, 23).

What type of music should they listen to and what

type should they not listen to? What type of clothing should they wear and what should they avoid? These are important issues they need to resolve. The apostle Paul used the cultural issue of meat offered to idols and the practice of women wearing veils to teach the Corinthians that an action in and of itself may not be wrong but the message portrayed by an action, within a particular culture at a particular time, may be wrong. Teens must learn this principle.

5. Substance Use & Abuse

Teens are the target of a lot of substance use and abuse. Many of their friends use alcohol, cigarettes, and drugs and boast of the pleasures associated with them. There may be pleasure in those things, but it is short lived (Heb. 11:25) and the effects those substances have on them can be devastating. Teens can be ostracized from the group if they don't smoke, drink or use some drugs. They need to know how to deal with this. This is a very real problem in both the urban, suburban, and rural community. There is no escaping it anymore.

6. Parent-Teen Relationships

For some teens the parent-teen relationship presents some very real struggles. A Christian home doesn't exempt a teen from this issue. Lack of understanding or proper biblical training on either part can cause some serious friction. Simple misunderstandings can turn into serious conflicts. An important issue is to help teens and parents learn to deal with their relationship.

7. Authority Relationships

Young people are learning how to relate to authority and leadership. The more people in leadership over young people, the harder it is for them to relate. When other adults in their lives question leadership, teens find it more difficult to accept leadership and learn to relate to it.

8. *Friends*

Friends are not only an influence but an issue in teens' lives. What type of friends should they have? What should they do with their friends? What do they do when their friends want to do something they shouldn't do, but they don't want to lose their friends?

Parents who try to isolate their teens from "the negative influence of unsaved teens" would be surprised to discover the sometimes more devastating "negative influence of saved teens."

9. *Dating*

Dating is an important issue to teens. They want to be with members of the opposite sex and will find ways to do it if opportunities are not provided.

When should a teen start to date? Who should they date? How do they ask someone for a date? What should they do on a date and where should they go? These are all questions teens need answered. What about going steady, engagement, marriage? Some teens look for security in a dating relationship and determine their self-acceptance based upon whether or not they have a date lined up for Friday night.

Promiscuity and immorality have become a real problem for teens. Immorality is heralded on television and glamorized in the movies and entertainment industry. The world confuses love and sex and expects both, outside of God's order. They center on the pleasure associated with sex and say little of the pain and scars it brings when fulfilled outside of God's plan. The pressure is intense both among saved and unsaved teens. According to surveys, the majority of teens have been involved in premarital sex by the time they finish high school, *including Christian teens.*

The acceptance of an immoral standard has legitimized abortion, the murder of an unborn child for the convenience of the mother. Many teens have had abortions and their parents do not even now about it.

Teens need a youth ministry which promotes godly guidelines for dating and one which provides opportunities to date. Dating can be a wonderful experience for teens or it can be one which scars them for life.

10. Facing the Future

What will I do with my life? That is a question teens must ask themselves. The teen years are the best time to begin to think about the future and make preparations for it. Certain classes taken in high school will help better prepare someone for a particular field of study. Colleges often base their acceptance criteria on a student's academic performance. Grade point averages for admission are often based on averages from ninth through eleventh grade. Many students are accepted by a school before they complete their senior year. The senior year of high school is often too late to think about entering some fields.

Scholarships for schooling are often based on a combination of academics and community involvement. The jobs a student holds and the after-school activities, such as their involvement in their church and youth ministry, can make the difference in qualifying for certain scholarships.

11. Working

Should a teen work after school, on weekends or during the summer? Some do it to earn spending money. Some do it to save for college. Others do it for experience to prepare them for the future.

Having a job can be a very positive experience for a teen, especially for those who grow up in a non-agricultural society or in a family which doesn't have a family business. Many teens don't have much responsibility. They could learn the importance of sticking to a schedule and the importance of the work ethic. A job can help build their confidence when they see what they can accomplish and also be paid for it at the same time.

A job can also have negative results. It could take away important study time. It could expose them to a host of negative influences they may not be prepared to handle. It could take them away from important church activities. It could put a lot more money in their hands than they know how to deal with properly.

12. Teen Suicide

The compounded effect of the various influences in the lives of teens and the issues they must face drive a number of teens to attempt to remove all the pressures from their lives. It is alarming how many teens resort to attempting suicide and even more alarming how many succeed.

Teens need help coping with the pressures and demands in their lives. They also need help coping with the death of a friend who has resorted to suicide.

Teenagers need someone like you who will take the time to learn to understand them. If more youth workers would make such a commitment, more teens would be reached and ministered to more effectively.

CHAPTER TWO

CHAPTER TWO
Essential Elements for Effective Youth Ministry

You Can Have an Effective Youth Ministry

There are a number of different ways you can help create an effective youth ministry in your church. You could become part of an organized club program like AWANA or Word of Life. These provide you with materials, planning calendars, training conferences, regional activities, and personnel to assist you. Or you could purchase a program from your Christian bookstore or organizations like Campus Life or Pro Teens. These usually include suggested meetings, lesson outlines, devotionals, and plans for activities. If you are creative, or if you have a limited budget, you could develop your own program. A leaders packet is available from Church Growth Institute to help you take the principles from this book and start a dynamic youth ministry using any of the youth programs mentioned above, or to help you develop your own program.

No matter what route you choose to follow, be sure the program you use includes the eight essential elements for effective youth ministry.

Before we look at those eight essential elements it is important for you to understand what I call the Principle of Emotional Separation.

The Principle of Emotional Separation

The Principle of Emotional Separation will help you understand the reason behind many of the methods used in youth ministry.

While a child is in its mother's womb, it is totally dependent on her for its existence. As soon as the child is born it begins its path to independence. The amount of dependence a child has on its mother, and ultimately on its parents, decreases over the years. This dependence is both physical and emotional.

Parents must remember that children don't belong to them, they are loaned to them by God to raise for Him (Ps. 127:3; Gen. 33:5; Prov. 22:6). The parents are responsible to raise their children to the point where they can stand alone.

God explained it this way, "Therefore shall a man leave his father and his mother and shall cleave unto his wife: and they shall be one flesh" (Gen. 2:24).

This leaving and cleaving involves both physical and emotional separation from their parents. Parents must begin to prepare their children and themselves for that separation. If done properly this process will be smooth for both the child and the parent.

The physical separation is inevitable. A child can't sit in your lap all his or her life. One day a child will sit and play alone. One day he or she will want to play with other children. Eventually the child will go off to school, perhaps off to college, then may even decide to move out on his or her own or decide to get married. This all involves physical separation.

Coupled with this physical separation must be emotional separation. The child must learn it is all right not to sit on your lap all of the time. He or she must feel emotionally secure to sit and play alone, to play with other children, to go off to school or to handle any other form of physical separation.

Parents must understand the need for the physical separation milestones in their child's life and must prepare themselves and their child for the emotional separation which accompanies them.

Physical Separation WITHOUT
Emotional Separation Preparation

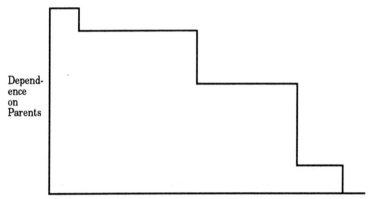

Depend-
ence
on
Parents

Milestones   Conception Birth Nursery Grade Junior High   College Marriage
                                         School High School

Physical Separation WITH
Emotional Separation Preparation

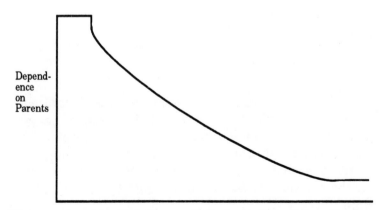

Depend-
ence
on
Parents

Milestones   Conception Birth Nursery Grade Junior High   College Marriage
                                         School High School

A tremendous problem occurs when parents do not understand this principle of emotional separation and do not want to let go of their children. When parents hold on as long as they can, each milestone becomes a time of great emotional upheaval.

In the end, such a parent either ends up with a child who grows up and becomes an adult but never leaves home because he or she is unprepared to handle the emotional separation, or they end up with a child who rebels against their possessiveness and possibly runs away from home or moves out as soon as possible, never to return home again.

If we handle emotional separation properly, children will grow up to stand on their own but will always remember their roots and will come home to visit when they can.

Emotional separation begins the first Sunday the child comes to church after getting out of the hospital. The parents must learn to trust the church nursery workers and place the child in their care during the service. It may be hard to let go of that cuddly helpless little child for that hour or two but it is the first step in emotional separation.

As the child grows he or she will learn church is a good place to be. Soon he or she will develop relationships with other children and even with the adult workers.

As the child goes off to school there is a significant amount of physical separation which requires a good measure of emotional separation. That separation will not be as hard on the parents who have had their child in the church nursery and Sunday School as it will be for the mother who has keep the child by her side all the time.

During those early school years comes other opportunities for physical separation which are part of the growing up process. There's little league or soccer, the children's program at church, staying overnight at a friend's house, and the real pull, a week at camp and perhaps even two weeks the next year.

A parent who learns to integrate these experiences in the life of their child, while maintaining a warm, loving home life, will help smooth the emotional separation necessary. The transitions become smooth rather than times of great emotional upheaval. There may be tears in the parents eyes that first day their child goes off to school, but it is not an emotional upheaval for those who prepare.

As children enter their teen years, they are in that final period before they go out on their own. They will want to be away from their parents more and more. That desire for separation is natural and healthy – it is preparing them for adulthood and the day they must stand alone.

The after-school activities, the part-time job, and even the youth ministry all play an important role in emotional separation. The week at camp may have grown to a month in a leadership training program. Some teens may even dedicate their entire summer to being away on missionary work.

There will definitely be a tug at your heart as you cross each one of these steps, but you can make the transition a smooth one for both you and your child, knowing you are training them up for the Lord.

When graduation comes and children go off to college, they will come home again if they have been prepared for the physical separation, with proper utilization of the emotional separation principle.

Then one day they will come home to tell you they've found the one they want to be their lifetime partner. You can rejoice when the day of separation comes. As you let them go, step by step, you reserve a special place in their hearts for you.

This Principle of Emotional Separation is very important for youth workers to understand. Possessive parents will try to make you feel guilty for doing so much with their teens. On the other hand, parents who don't realize they still have responsibility to still spend time with their teens will complain that you don't do enough with them.

If you realize the importance of the youth ministry in emotional separation and understand what the parents and teens are going through, you and your ministry will be better. Then be sure your program includes the following eight essential elements for effective youth ministry.

The Eight Essential Elements for Effective Youth Ministry

After more than 20 years of experience in youth work I have found that no matter what type of youth program you have the following eight elements are essential for effective youth ministry.

1. Dedicated Workers

You need dedicated workers to start a dynamic youth ministry. Though it would be helpful to have some teens and more than one worker, just one person dedicated to the Lord and to the task of reaching and teaching teens is all it takes to start a dynamic youth ministry. A dedicated worker will find teens to minister to and will make a difference in their lives.

To make a difference in the lives of young people for all eternity, dedicated youth workers must have a daily walk with God, not just *know about* God. Youth workers must have a personal living relationship with Jesus Christ. They must spend time with God in prayer and reading the Word each day, then they must apply the truths they learn from Scripture to their lives.

They must *depend on God for wisdom and strength.* If they realize their inadequacies they will seek what they need from God who will gladly equip them for the task.

The dedicated youth worker will work at understanding teens and will seek effective means of ministering to the total person: body, soul, and spirit (1 Thess. 5:23).

2. Evangelism

The second essential element for an effective youth ministry is evangelism, the first part of the Great Commission. Evangelism has been called by some, "the heartbeat of God." Evangelism is the lifeblood of the church. Without evangelism a church eventually dies and so does a youth ministry.

The first part of the Great Commission (Matt. 28:19-20; Mark 16:15) gives us a charge to go into the all the world and bring the Gospel, the good news of salvation in Christ and all that entails, to every creature.

For your youth ministry to be effective in God's eyes it must seek to evangelize young people. Your goal should be to take the Gospel to each teen in your community in a meaningful and effective way, not just to work with the teens you have.

An effective youth ministry will not only reach out to young people but will also equip its young people and provide them with opportunities to reach other young people for the Lord. In essence it encourages *youth to be reaching youth.*[1]

Evangelism is more than just presenting the Gospel or getting decisions. It involves following up on those you reach. Your youth ministry needs a way to follow up on those contacted or reached through the evangelistic aspect of your program.

3. Teaching & Preaching

The third essential element for an effective youth ministry is the second aspect to the Great Commission. You need to *teach* the Word of God and biblical principles to those you reach. This is done through teaching and preaching.

Teaching and preaching are different from each other but are closely related. Teaching is imparting knowledge, preaching is taking information and making the application. Teaching can involve preaching and preaching can involve teaching. Both are important.

You need to determine what you want to teach your young people. What information do they need? Make a specific list of what they need to know.

Then determine what to preach. You obviously should preach the Gospel during evangelistic aspects of your program. Preaching is an effective means God has given for evangelism (1 Cor. 1:21).

All preaching is not evangelistic. A lot of preaching should be geared toward applying biblical principles to daily living. A devotional is preaching.

Determine who should teach or preach in your youth ministry. Many people would like to teach or preach, but you must be careful who does. Your church should have a policy regarding who can teach or preach. Remember, a person's life gives them a platform for teaching.

Determine how to teach or preach. Not all teaching or preaching is effective, but it can be. The teaching and preaching process in essence requires a person with *a message, using a method to reach another person.*

Though there are messages which are appropriate for any age group, young people have specific needs which require specific teaching and preaching. They also have certain age-group characteristics, such as attention span, which necessitate that the message be delivered in such a way that it keeps their attention and is easily understood.

Teachers and preachers would be amazed if they realized how many people receive so little of their message because of their methods.

4. Discipleship

The fourth essential element for an effective youth ministry is discipleship, the third part of the Great Commission.

Discipleship takes students beyond salvation and instruction and helps them make specific application of the principles of Scripture to their daily lives.

Though teaching and preaching help in the discipleship process, the most effective form of discipleship is one on one. When an older believer shows a personal interest in a younger believer, they open the door for effective discipleship.

Discipleship can be very structured, using books, curriculum and a specific plan, or it can be casual, with the discipler identifying the greatest areas of needs in the disciple's life and sharing how the need can be met by applying biblical principles. No matter what discipleship method your youth ministry uses it should help the teens develop good spiritual habits, then provide them opportunity to put to use what they have learned.

At first the youth leader may do most of the discipling but soon others will be trained and can teach the things they have learned (2 Tim. 2:2).

5. Activity

The fifth essential element for an effective youth ministry is activity. Young people love and need lots of activity.

God did not design teens to sit around and listen to your teaching or preaching all the time. Activities are a great way to provide not only recreation and dating opportunities for your teens but also to provide opportunities for service and a way to help you see what your teens have learned and what they still need to learn.

There are basically three different kinds of activities: *outreach* activities, where the thrust is to reach the unsaved teen; *our* activities, where the thrust is to provide recreation and dating opportunities for your teens; and *others* activities, where the thrust is on reaching out to minister to other groups of people.

A carefully planned activity calendar will include all three types of activities for your teens.

6. *Counseling*

The sixth essential element for an effective youth ministry is counseling. The Bible says we are not just to teach those we work with but we are to *admonish* them as well (Col. 3:16). Admonishing means to counsel others using the Word of God.

Teens need someone they can go to for counsel. They also need someone who will care enough to go to them when they need counseling but don't seek it. They need help and guidance in dealing with personal problems. When someone is overtaken by a problem, sometimes they have a hard time seeing how to apply the solution to the problem. Someone who genuinely cares about teens will help guide them to the solution to their problems so they can apply it and experience victory in Jesus.

Teens also need counsel as they seek direction and make various decisions in their lives. A youth ministry needs to help them with personal direction and vocational counseling.

Jay Adams has written several books to help Christian workers effectively counsel those they work with.

7. *Organization & Administration*

The seventh essential element for an effective youth ministry is organization and administration. God is not the author of confusion. He wants things done in an orderly fashion (1 Cor. 14:33, 40). That means leaders must pay attention to administrative details (Eph. 4:11-16).

Some youth ministries lack organization and flounder or are not effective with organizational details like promotion, transportation, follow-up and record-keeping. They could function more effectively if they were more organized.

An effective ministry will keep various records, such as attendance, visitation, and financial records. It takes organization and careful planning to draft a budget for a youth ministry to function on the limited funds often available to it.

Organization helps to see that all aspects of the youth ministry are coordinated among themselves and with the rest of the church.

For a youth ministry to develop the leadership team it needs to grow and for it to maintain a balanced program, it must be organized with a time and a purpose for everything.

8. *Evaluation*

The eighth essential element for an effective youth ministry is evaluation. Many ministries do the same thing year after year and never evaluate it to see if it is effective.

Effectiveness, in God's eyes, is not just how many do you have in your youth ministry today, but where are they and what are they doing tomorrow. The fruit which remains is what counts (1 Cor. 3:10-14).

Every aspect of our youth ministry must be evaluated, from the activities to the teachings. If something works, you need to ask, what made it work? If something does not work you need to ask, why didn't it work?

If you remember the principle of emotional separation and seek to incorporate all eight of the essential elements for effective youth ministry in your teen program, you can have a dynamic youth ministry no matter what program you use.

FOOTNOTES

[1] A great tool to use to motivate and involve youth in evangelistic outreach is the *TEAM Mate* (youth version), published by Church Growth Institute.

CHAPTER THREE

CHAPTER THREE
The Leadership Team

Team Ministry & Spiritual Gifts

To have an efficient, growing youth ministry, a leadership team must be developed. At first you may be the only member on that team, but if you want your ministry to grow you need to prepare others to become part of your leadership team.

Team ministry is a biblical concept. A careful study of the Acts of the Apostles and the epistles will reveal that ministry teams were the norm in the New Testament. Barnabas took Paul with him as part of his ministry team (Acts 13:1-3). Then later, when Paul led his own team he took Silas with him (Acts 15:40). My most effective ministry to teens has always been when I was able to pull together and train a team of leaders to work with me.

The reason we are more effective as a team is because the Lord has given each believer a spiritual gift and made us a part of His body, the church (Rom. 12:4-5). Just as our physical bodies have different parts with different functions, so too the body of Christ (the church) has different parts with different functions. The Bible says, some are like an eye, others like an ear. Each part needs the others to minister effectively (1 Cor. 12:12-27).

If we try to conduct our ministry independently as individuals we will miss out on certain aspects of ministry which would produce a more effective program. Imagine if your whole body were a hand. You can do a lot with a hand. You may even be able to walk on your hands. But it would be more effective if the hand did what hands are best at and found a pair of feet to do the walking. The same is true in ministry.

Each person on your ministry team will bring with them a gift which gives them a unique perspective on ministry and unique abilities which can be developed and used effectively in different facets of the ministry.

The Holy Spirit gives us our spiritual gift, the Lord Jesus gives us a ministry where we can use our gift, and the Father gives the results (1 Cor. 12:4-6). What a joy to know we do not have to produce the results. God gives the results as we faithfully use our gift in ministry for Him.

Understanding that you have a gift which God gives you to use in ministry for Him will help you realize you can be effective in ministry because God has thereby equipped you to serve Him through this gift. Then you must learn what your gift is.

Understanding the fact that there are different gifts, and thus different perspectives on ministry and different abilities, will help you to realize the need to accept the different ways different people look at ministry. This will help coordinate the team as the Lord brings you together to serve Him. This will help you have a more balanced ministry which can minister to the total person.

A person with the gift of prophesy, whose joy is to convince others of right and wrong, will have a different perspective on ministry than the person with the gift of mercy, whose joy is to comfort others and create an atmosphere for service. These two gifts in particular are almost opposites but both would bring two different, yet necessary, perspectives to your ministry team.

To pull together the most effective ministry team, look for people who have a different spiritual gift than you. Then, when you hold team meetings where you develop your plans and strategy, be sure each team member gives their input. This will give you the broadest possible perspective on your ministry and will help you identify the strengths and weaknesses of your program and make the appropriate changes.

Though each gift could be used in a variety of ministries, try to match the worker with the ministry which gives them the best opportunity to minister their gift. Prophets need a ministry where they can speak, mercy-showers need a ministry where they can counsel and minister to the needs of others. In your team meetings you can identify who will best serve in what position.

Opportunities for Service in Local Church Youth Ministry

There are numerous opportunities for service in a local church youth ministry. In a new or smaller ministry some people will need to fulfill two or more positions. As your ministry grows, your need for more workers will grow and individuals may be able to concentrate on one aspect of the ministry.

Teens should also be involved in service in your youth ministry. They could do some jobs some adults normally do. We will look at that more closely in another chapter.

The following are some of the opportunities for service in youth ministry:

1. Youth Pastor/Youth Director

Someone must be responsible to lead the youth ministry. In some churches that person is a professionally trained youth pastor. There is a lot to say for professional training in this field. A youth pastor is as much a pastor to those he ministers to as the senior pastor is to those he ministers to. Most churches would never think of calling a pastor without professional training.

Though a professionally trained youth pastor may be the ideal, some churches are not able to have one because of size or budget. The task of directing the youth ministry often falls to a layperson. The term "director," in church nomenclature, implies a trained non-professional layperson directing a ministry.

Whether you have a youth pastor or youth director, someone has to lead the youth ministry in your church.

The one who leads the youth ministry should co-ordinate the other workers. This person is both re-sponsible and accountable for how the youth ministry functions and should therefore have the final say on all decisions.

For the smoothest operation and to have as effective a youth ministry as possible, all aspects of the youth ministry in the church should flow through this person. That includes youth meetings, youth activities, teen Sunday School, youth sports programs, summer mis-sions, camp and retreats, teen choir and anything else involving teens.

Other people may head up particular aspects of the church's ministry to teens but they must be accountable to one person who heads up the youth ministry, in the same way that all ministries involving adults are ac-countable to the senior pastor.

Obviously the larger the church and more diverse the ministry, the more training the youth pastor/youth director needs. If that training has not been secured in Bible college it must be secured through reading, ob-servation, conferences and seminars, and on-the-job training.

2. Sunday School/Bible Study Teacher

A dynamic youth ministry really needs a Sunday School or Bible Study program for its teens. A good teen Sunday School program can be one of the greatest as-sets to your youth ministry.

If you have a smaller church with limited facilities

and limited workers when you start your youth ministry, it may not be possible to have a teen Sunday School class. Your teens may have to be part of another class at first. Even so, they need the identity as the teen class and need someone to rally them together. One of your goals should be to develop a teen Sunday School or Bible Study program as soon as possible.

As your youth ministry grows, it will need more than one Sunday School class. You will probably want to separate the junior high from the senior high first. Then you will probably want to offer some separate boys and girls classes from time to time, so you can deal with issues particular to each group which would not be appropriate or effective to deal with in mixed company.

I advise against dividing your teen Sunday School into separate classes for different grades. Group dynamics work best when teaching teens. There is also an esprit d'corps which forms when you meet as a group.

If you want to have some small group instruction time, I recommend scheduling elective classes at different times throughout the year, dividing the class into discussion groups or assigning them to small group projects from time to time during regular group classes.

A good teen program needs teachers. You may be the only teacher at first. Your job is to prepare lessons which minister to the needs in the lives of your young people and to follow up on your students.

Every teacher should have a regular visitation plan. A good rule of thumb regarding visitation is to visit every visitor and contact every absentee every week, visit every regular attender once a semester, and contact prospects regularly.

As a teacher your job is also to train other teachers (2 Tim. 2:2). Every teacher should have an assistant who is actually a teacher in training.

3. Workers/Leaders

Every youth ministry needs workers. Workers are those who work with the director to carry out various aspects of the program. They may coordinate a whole area of the ministry or they may be responsible for one particular aspect or function. Usually they do more than one thing in the youth ministry. These are the active members of the leadership team.

If at all possible, it is best for youth workers not to be parents of teens. Teens need a break from their parents and parents need a break from their teens. Teens whose parents work in the program tend to act differently than they would if their parents weren't around. You can use parents of teens from time to time, but I have found it works best if they are not the regular leaders.

Youth workers also function as chaperones for your activities but you should never refer to workers as chaperones. Teens resent the idea of being chaperoned. They don't think of the youth workers or drivers as chaperones unless they are called such.

Never make a public appeal for youth workers or drivers for your teen program unless you are prepared to handle volunteers who you do not want working with your teens.

4. Assistants & Auxiliary Workers

Every youth worker needs an assistant. From the Sunday School teacher to the person coordinating refreshments, assistants are valuable assets.

There are formal assistants and informal assistants. **Formal assistants** are actually leaders in training, being groomed for a spot on the leadership team. A formal assistant may teach or bring a devotional or even lead an activity as part of their training. The standards and commitment for a formal assistant should be the same as for regular workers.

An **informal assistant** is someone who helps from time to time. It would be better to call these **auxiliary workers.** The commitment and standards for an auxiliary worker would not need to be as high as that for a youth worker or for a formal assistant. Auxiliary workers would never teach or bring a devotional but would help in other areas wherever and whenever they are needed.

5. Drivers

Every youth ministry needs drivers. You need drivers to get teens to and from your program. You also need drivers from time to time to drive for your activities. Good drivers are a valuable resource.

Determine policies about who can drive for an activity. One of the most dangerous places for teens is in a car. Some youth ministries set policies as to who can drive others to and from their youth programs.

If you minister to average teenagers, you will have some whose parents do not set proper standards for their teens. A lot of immorality and sin takes place in cars on the way to or from many youth ministries. Sometimes it is never planned but often it happens. Many good teenagers could be spared unnecessary scars if youth leaders would set policies about driving.

Not everyone is qualified to drive for a youth activity. Some people are not safe drivers. Some drivers may have habits or language you do not want your teens around. Some drivers may not have the patience to drive for teens. Teens should be allowed to have a good time on the way to and from an activity or anytime they are in a car for an activity. Some people cannot handle the laughing and silly jokes younger teens are especially fond of.

Drivers have an opportunity to minister to teens in their car. They should be an example by their words and deeds. They should also be able to guide a conversation or activity in the car, especially if things get too quiet or if they get out of hand.

6. Hosts

As a part of a dynamic youth ministry you will want to have meetings and activities in homes from time to time. The same principles for drivers apply for those who open up their homes for your youth ministry.

Some people have family rooms, large living rooms, patios or large yards which make an excellent place for some aspect of your program. If you have a church with rented or limited facilities you may want to use a home as a base for your weekly youth meeting or youth activities.

The youth pastor should visit and approve of any home you intend to use in your ministry to be sure the hosts are the type of people you want your teens around.

Those who open their homes need to realize that having teens in their home is not like having adults around. Some teens forget to wipe the mud off their boots, others may wear clothing which is not very clean. Almost anytime there are refreshments, at least one of the teens will spill something. Teens can take a toll on a house.

Sometimes hosts should be part of the program. For some aspects of your program the host may open their house but not actually participate in your program. Some hosts are very glad to do that. This is something you need to make clear to start with.

Usually hosts will be around when it comes time for refreshments. Providing refreshments is another way hosts can be helpful. Be sure to inform them if refreshments are needed, what your preference is, and if other refreshments will be brought along.

7. Secretarial & Financial

Every youth ministry needs someone to take care of the secretarial and financial details. The youth pastor may need to be the one doing this at first. The sooner someone is chosen to handle these details, the better. This person should be good with details.

As your program grows, the need for additional secretarial and financial personnel will grow too. These people are very valuable members of your leadership team.

Keep attendance records, information on each teen for follow-up and visitation (counseling records are confidential), a planning calendar, and a record of income and expenses. Someone should also keep the minutes at your leadership team meetings.

A designated secretary could help with correspondence and administrative details involved in planning and costing out various items for your program.

8. Promotional

Often the youth director or secretary ends up handling the promotional work at first. This is a great area in which to involve someone with either artistic ability, graphic arts skills or public relations background.

You need to get the word out about your youth ministry to both your teens and to the teens in the community. Posters, flyers, new releases, ads and newsletters are all excellent promotional tools. A person with creativity can do a lot to promote your youth ministry.

This also includes taking pictures or videos of your activities for future promotion or for your youth ministry yearbook.

9. Campus Leader

If your church includes a campus ministry as part of your youth ministry, campus leaders are needed. These are often a cross between a Sunday School teacher, youth director and host who either goes on a campus to direct a campus teen club or hosts such an after-school club in their home. They usually meet in the afternoon after school, or on a weeknight in a home near the school.

Campus clubs are effective if you are in an area where the teens in your church attend various schools. In an area where it is not feasible for teens to come from other schools to your church or youth ministry, you can conduct one campus-type club meeting for all your teens.

The campus leader usually serves as both host and teacher. In some cases the host and campus leader may be a different person.

Some programs like AWANA, Pro Teens, and Word of Life are excellent for campus clubs. If you do not have enough leaders for one of those programs, you can still have a campus club ministry with just one worker by adapting other materials and following the principles found in this book's chapter on youth meetings.

10. Sports or Game Coordinator

A dynamic youth ministry always has some form of activity for the teens. At first the youth pastor may be the one who coordinates the game part of your program. However, it would be helpful for someone else to do this.

Too often an athlete is put in charge of the games and they end up being geared only for the athletic. When game time becomes a basketball game week after week, those who don't like basketball or who don't excel at the game don't enjoy it and often stop coming.

The games at your activities must be something both the athletic and nonathletic will enjoy. The game director should understand the principle of equalizer activities explained in the chapter on activities.

Some churches have enough teens to have a sports program where a team of teens play against other churches in a particular sport. Some youth ministries develop mini-leagues in their own community to reach other teens. If you have such a program, a coordinator must be chosen to work with the youth director. Remember that such a program should never be the primary focus of your youth ministry because it only ministers to one segment of teens.

Qualifications for Youth Workers

Though challenges and struggles exist in youth ministry, working with teens can be a rewarding and often a very enjoyable experience. Some people will see the fun and excitement associated with youth ministry and will want to work with your teens, but should not.

Every youth ministry needs qualifications which workers should meet if they want to work with teens. Some churches have established standards for all workers. Those standards should be adhered to by all youth workers. In addition, I have found it helpful to have youth workers meet the following qualifications:

1. Member of Your Church

Each worker must understand the need to be a member of a local body of believers so they can function effectively as a part of that body.

The unwillingness of a potential worker to become part of your church could be a sign of a rebellious heart which doesn't want to submit to the authority of the local church.

If your youth workers are not members of your church, they will not be convinced to encourage the young people they reach to become part of your church.

2. Have Personal Holiness

Youth workers must be born-again believers who are striving to walk with the Lord every day. They should spend time in personal devotions daily and should seek to apply the principles they learn to their daily walk.

3. Have a Burden to Work with Teens

Too many people, especially recent Bible college graduates whose ultimate goal is to become a senior pastor, use the youth ministry as a stepping stone. I would rather have one layperson willing to learn and who is dedicated to working with teens than a room full of professionals who want experience for their resumes so they can have a better chance at becoming pastors. I don't mind giving someone experience working with me, but I want to know that and I would want my teens to know that up front.

Teens know when they are being used as stepping stones. They can also recognize when a person genuinely cares for them. A person doesn't have to be young, good looking, and energetic to work with teens. A person who has a heart for teens will do whatever it takes to be effective in ministry with them and the teens will respond positively to that.

4. Have a Servant's Heart

Those who want to work with teens must have a servant's heart. They must understand the principle of submission to authority and work within a chain of command.

Mavericks who have great abilities will only be a detriment to your program. They must allow the Lord to break their will and learn to work under God-given authority.

A person with a servant's heart will recognize their inadequacies and will be willing to learn. That is an essential ingredient for a good youth worker.

5. Understand the Need to Work With and Train Others

Youth workers must understand they have to work with others to be effective in youth ministry. Some people work well under a chain of command but do not work well with others. This is usually due to improper training or an improper understanding of the gifts of the Spirit. If they are willing to learn to work with others they can be a valuable asset.

Youth workers must also understand the 2 Timothy 2:2 principle which says every worker must be training others. No matter what we are called to do, we are to teach others to do it too.

6. Have Spirit Control & Self-Control

Youth workers must depend on the wisdom and power of the Holy Spirit to be effective in ministry. They must recognize the arm of flesh will fail them but the Spirit never will.

They must also have self-control. There are a lot of tempting situations in youth work which require the youth workers' self-control. Teens also need to see adults who exhibit self-control, an area of real struggle in many teens' lives.

A person with Spirit control and self-control will have godly standards for their life and will understand the principle of appropriateness. They will recognize there is a time and a place for everything.

7. *Willing to Pay the Price*

Any youth leader must recognize there is a price to pay to be involved in youth work.

There is a demand for their **time**. The commitment to work with teens includes preparation time, time at the program, follow-up time, and being available at odd hours.

There is a demand for their **talents**. Most youth ministries need all of their workers to perform more than one duty. Youth workers need to develop and use all of their talents for the Lord.

There is also a demand for their **treasure.** Most youth ministries are insufficiently funded. Youth workers will find themselves reaching deep into their own pockets to minister in a variety of ways.

When a church understands the concept of team ministry (recognizing that each believer has a gift which can be used in ministry), identifies the opportunities for putting gifts to work in youth ministry, and finds workers who are willing to allow the Lord to conform them to the qualifications for service, it can and will have a dynamic ministry to teens.

CHAPTER FOUR

CHAPTER FOUR
Developing Christian Character in Young People

Discipleship Is Essential

Our main goal in youth work is to reach young people with the Gospel of Jesus Christ, then help them grow in Him. Some type of discipleship program is essential to do that.

One of the first youth ministries in which I worked overemphasized the evangelism aspect of youth work and neglected the discipleship of its converts. Evangelism is important, but without the instruction on how to grow in Christ, most of those converts fall away. That ministry died out in a few years and had little long-lasting impact.

We must remember to follow the Great Commission (Matt. 28:19-20). It tells us to evangelize *and* disciple.

In your youth ministry, discipleship will help you develop Christian character in your young people. This requires a combination of one-on-one involvement and effective practical group teaching through the instructional aspects of your program.

What Is Christian Character?

Growing up as a Christian teen, I was given the following advice on how to be spiritual: "Don't drink, don't smoke, don't chew, and don't go out with girls that do." That is sound advice, but it doesn't make someone spiritual.

I never had a desire to go out with girls that chewed (tobacco), but that wasn't for spiritual reasons. I did go out with girls who, I later found out, drank and smoked. The surprising thing was, those girls weren't any less spiritual than some of the girls who didn't do those things. In fact, I often saw a spiritual snobbery shown by those who prided themselves on "I don't do this" or "I don't do that."

It is interesting to learn how many who "don't do this or that" either have done it behind closed doors, wish they could or would do it if they could. A lot of Christian parents would be surprised if they really knew everything their teens have done, are doing or would like to do.

Even though a teen may follow the advice to abstain from certain practices, it does not guarantee that he or she is spiritual. Too often we gauge spirituality by what people *do*, rather than by what they *are*. It is possible to change what people *do* but not what they *are*. Though good behavior is a desirable characteristic, and one which should be seen in all good Christians, good behavior is not necessarily the mark of a good Christian.

Christian character is what a person *is*. Our goal should be to change what a person is. That in turn will change what they *do*.

If young people are convinced of what to do and why to do it, and make those choices based on biblical principles rather than on someone else's code of conduct for them, they will do what they ought to do and won't do what they shouldn't do, because they will *be* what they ought to be.

What are some of the characteristics you would like to see in your young people? Make a list of them. You must identify these so you can set out to help develop them in the lives of young people.

In 1 Timothy 4:12, the apostle Paul identified some characteristics he wanted to see developed in young Timothy.

"Let no man despise thy youth; but be thou an example of the believers, in word, in conversation, in charity, in spirit, in faith, in purity."

Word – God wants our teens to be careful about what they say. The tongue is a tool that can be used for great good or much evil (James 3:1-10). There are some things teens need to learn not to say and other things they need to learn when to say (Eph. 4:15, 29). This can save them from a lot of trouble, help them say the right things, and help them see others saved.

Conversation – This is an old word which indicates our entire lifestyle. Our conversation is the way we conduct ourselves on a day-to-day basis. Teens need to know God is concerned about the little daily tasks they undertake (Col. 3:17). They need to learn how to involve God in every area of their lives. This will help them to do the things pleasing in the sight of both God and man.

Charity – Love for others is one of the true marks of a Christian (John 13:34-35; 1 Thess. 3:12-13). Teens need to learn to allow God to develop a love in their hearts motivated by what they can give, not what they can get. This will help them find true spiritual and emotional fulfillment.

Spirit – This is the word for enthusiasm. Young people are full of enthusiasm. They need to know God wants them to be enthusiastic for Him. He wants them to be full of His joy (John 15:11). This will help them live the abundant Christian life.

Faith – We are saved through faith (Eph. 2:8-9) and grow in Christ through faith (Rom. 1:17). Faith has substance and is evidence of God's working in our lives (Heb. 11:1). Young people need to strengthen their faith and learn to live by faith. This will help them face any struggle which comes their way and will help them do great things for God.

Purity – God wants to use each young person. He wants to set them apart from the damaging influences of sin and wants to fill them with His Spirit so they can know the fulness of life and live a life pleasing to Him (1 Thess. 5:23; Col. 3:16). This will help keep them morally, physically, and spiritually pure.

How can you develop such Christian character in the lives of your young people? Paul answered that question in the same context. In 1 Timothy 4:13, he said, "Till I come, give attendance to reading, to exhortation, to doctrine." These three things will help develop Christian character in the lives of your young people and should be part of your discipleship program:

Reading – For anyone to grow as a Christian and to develop the type of Christian character God wants them to have they need to develop the habit of having a personal time of devotions with the Lord each day. They need to read God's Word and spend time in prayer (Josh. 1:8; Ps. 1).

Exhortation – Everyone needs someone else to encourage them and help challenge them to grow in the Lord (Heb. 10:22-25). This needs to be done individually, one on one, and corporately as a church and youth ministry.

Doctrine – What a person believes is important. We become what we believe ("As a man thinketh in his heart, so is he," Prov. 23:7). Paul stressed the importance of understanding good doctrine (1 Thess. 5:21; 2 Tim. 1:13; Phil. 2:16). Teens must be taught the Word of God in a way they can understand and apply it to their lives. It can give them the knowledge and discretion they need (Prov. 1:2-6).

Whether you use a formal discipleship program which you purchase or one which you develop yourself, be sure it includes reading, exhortation, and doctrine and you will see the fruit you desire in the lives of your young people.

Personal Interest

Some of the most effective discipleship is conducted one on one. At first the youth pastor and workers will have to do most of the personal discipleship work. After each person has been discipled, one can help disciple another and soon the amount of people involved in personal discipleship will multiply.

People want someone to take personal interest in them. Too often in a group situation many people never open up. They need that one-on-one interest shown in them. Taking that personal interest in someone can melt a cold heart.

I learned that principle when I was youth pastor in a church which had a Christian school, where I also worked. One of the teens would not come to the youth program nor would he do his work in school. One day he told me, "My father's the head deacon here and I don't need to do anything I don't want to do." He was a real challenge, but I knew somehow he could be reached. I asked the Lord for the wisdom to reach him.

One day I was planning a youth activity and needed to know where certain types of places were around town. I gave this teen a call and asked if he would be willing to show me around town. I told him we would stop for pizza along the way. He agreed to come and said it was because he didn't have anything else to do.

As we drove around town he began to open up more and more and the walls came down. We developed a friendship that day because of the personal time we had together. From that day on he started to do better in school, came regularly to our youth program and began to grow in the Lord.

A good standard to follow for personal discipleship is for men to disciple the teen guys and women to disciple the teen girls, until you have teens to do discipleship work. Even then you should be involved in discipling some. The principle of discipling those of the same sex will save you from potential problems and is very biblical (1 Thess. 5:22; Titus 2:1-8).

Developing Spiritual Habits

One very effective way to help your teens develop Christian character is to help them develop good spiritual habits.

1. Personal Devotions or Quiet Time

One of the most essential ingredients for developing Christian character is to have a personal time with God each day. Though God is with His children at all times, and though we can converse with Him anywhere and at anytime, we need a special time set aside when we read God's Word and spend some time in personal prayer each day.

I have found this to be the greatest key to my spiritual growth and to the growth of those I have had the opportunity to minister to and with.

Over the years I tried various methods of having a personal time with God but nothing seemed to work. I tried devotional books and booklets. I would start for a while but then I would quit. Finally, thanks to the exhortation of Lou Nichols, a long-time Word of Life missionary to teenagers (remember the apostle Paul stressed the importance of exhortation), I began to use a diary for my quiet time with God. It revolutionized my personal devotions. Everyday I began to write down what I read from God's Word and wrote down an application from the passage to my life. I also used a daily prayer list to pray for others.

This method works best when you make yourself accountable to someone else and let them ask to see your devotional diary at any time. It helps make sure you don't miss a day. In the process of developing this habit you begin to read the Word of God, purposefully looking to apply it to your life. At the end of a year you will have made 365 personal applications of the Word of God to your life.

There was an old saying written in the cover of my father's Bible which applies here. It said, "This book will keep you from sin, or sin will keep you from this book." Getting your teens in the Bible on a daily basis is one of the best things you can do for them. It will strengthen their personal walk with God and He will be able to teach them personally.

I recommend that teen workers follow the same format for their personal devotions as they recommend to their teens. Then make yourself accountable to the teens, allowing them to see your devotional diary any time and ask for the same from them. You will find it a very rewarding experience. It will help both you and your teens keep on your toes spiritually as it helps you all grow in the Lord.

2. Prayer

Besides having a daily time of reading God's Word, youth leaders and teens also need a daily time of prayer.

I used the simple prayer list concept for a number of years, then found another method which transformed my prayer time. Dan Knickerbocker, a pastor friend of mine, introduced it to me when he spoke for chapel at a college where I served as Dean. Pastor Knickerbocker recommended keeping a prayer diary.

Now I, my wife, and my teens all use our own personal prayer diaries. In the prayer diary we have prayer lists, divided by categories and days, along with places to record the answers to prayer.

I use a 9.5 inch by 6 inch three-ring binder, but an 8.5 inch by 5.5 inch one would work just as well. I open the notebook and turn over the first sheet of paper so I have the back of a page on the left and the front of the page on the right. I then use the left side for answers to prayer and the right side for the prayer requests or for listing names of people for whom I am praying.

Sample Prayer Diary – Format 1

Answered Prayer 1993 URGENT			URGENT	
		○	○	
Date	Answer		Date	Request
		○	○	

Sample Prayer Diary – Format 2

Answered Prayer 1993 Christian Friends			Christian Friends		
		○	○		
Date	Answer		Day	Name	Place
			Sun.		
			Mon.		
		○	○		

I use an individual sheet for each category and a corresponding page for each category of answers. When the paper on the left side (answers to prayer) fills up, I put it in the back of the book and insert another sheet for answers. This way, requests are always on the right hand side and answers on the left.

I use two different formats for the various categories. Format 1 is for requests to be prayed for daily: such as Urgent, Personal, Church and sheets for individual family members. Format 2 is for people I pray for once a week. Some Format 2 categories include: Relatives (Cousins, etc.), Christian Friends, Unsaved, Christian Workers, and World Leaders.

The Format 2 categories list names, not specific requests. Each day as you come to each name, pray for that person's physical and spiritual health, also pray for any specific needs you know of in their life. When you see them or hear from them you can write down the blessings of God in their lives as answers to prayer.

Each day I start at page one and pray my way through each of the sheets. It doesn't take very long but it is very productive. When you see people you can let them know you are praying for them (unless telling them so would offend them). At the end of the year you will have a written legacy which will have hundreds of answers to prayer recorded.

At the beginning of my prayer diary I have outlined each element in what has become known as the Lord's Prayer, Matthew 6:9-13, and pray for each item as follows:

"Our Father which art in Heaven"
 – Pray in a personal way.

"Hallowed be thy name"
 – Praise God for who He is.

"Thy kingdom come"
 – Pray for the Lord's return.

"Thy will be done in earth, as it is in heaven."
  – Pray for God's will to be done in my life today.

"Give us this day our daily bread"
  – Pray for daily provision.

"And forgive us our debts"
  – Pray for forgiveness of personal sin.

"As we forgive our debtors"
  – Pray for a forgiving spirit toward others.

"And lead us not into temptation"
  – Pray God will keep me from the place of temptation.

"But deliver us from evil"
  – Pray God will give me victory over evil today.

"For Thine is the kingdom, and the power, and the glory forever"
  – Praise God for who He is and for what He does.

If you pray through these personal items and pray using the prayer sheets you will be amazed how much more meaningful your prayer time becomes and how much better each day will be. You can spend as little as 15 minutes in prayer to as much as two hours as the Lord leads you. Start off with a little at first and you will want to spend more time in prayer as you see God work.

If you and your teens will use some type of method of praying for yourselves, for each other, and for others, every day, you will see God working in many ways and will grow in your Christian life.

3. *Church Attendance*

God designed the local church as the place where believers should assemble together to be taught the Word of God and to minister to one another (Heb. 10:19-25). God wants to pour down His glory upon the church (Eph. 3:21).

Your youth ministry must point to and get them involved *in* the local church in order to develop Christian character in their lives.

You will encourage them to be faithful to the church by your personal example. What you do speaks a lot louder than what you say.

If the services at your church are meaningful to your teens, they will come, with some encouragment.

There are a few ways you and your church can make the services more meaningful to your teens. The most effective way is to involve them in the service. Sing songs that appeal to teens along with your other music. Have teens pray in the service as you do adults. Include teens in your choir and use teens for special music. Have some teens serve as ushers. Encourage them to share testimonies.

You can also make the services more meaningful by discussing some aspect of the sermon in your youth program.

Another effective way to help the teens get more out of the sermon is by having sermon note sheets for them to fill out during the sermon as part of an incentive program.

We remember approximately:

10% of what we hear.

40% of what we hear and see.

90% of what we hear, see, and do.

Sample Sermon Note Form

Date_____ Place _____

Speaker_____

○ Sermon Title:_____

Main Scripture Passage_____

Main Points, Scripture, Illustrations

1.

2.

○
3.

Application (How Can I Apply This to My Life?):

4. *Christian Service*

Personal devotions, prayer, and church attendance will prepare your teens for one of the most important spiritual habits, that of Christian service. Every believer was saved to serve (Eph. 2:8-10). God has given each believer, including teens, a spiritual gift that should be used in spiritual service. As teens serve, they will grow.

Developing Leadership Qualities in Teens

As your teens develop Christian character you will find that some of them will make good leaders. As much as possible, you want to give them the opportunity to develop leadership qualities.

The church seems to be about the only institution which doesn't recognize the leadership potential in teens. Fast-food restaurants recognize it and allow them to become assistant managers. Politicians recognize it and allow them to work on their campaign staffs and be legislative aides. The Boy Scouts and Girls Scouts recognize it and allow them to spearhead community projects. It is time the church recognized the leadership potential of its young people and helped them develop biblical leadership qualities.

Leadership is something which is both *taught* and *caught*. It takes both instruction and involvement to learn leadership. To do this you need a specific time for training teens to be leaders and opportunities for them to put what they learn into use.

Consider having a special teen leadership meeting. This could be conducted the same night as the midweek prayer service at your church, before the evening service or before your regular youth meeting. This would be a time of sharing, praying, teaching, and planning. This may start with just you and one teen at first, but it should include other youth workers as they are added, as well as other teens who become interested in attending.

Responsibilities and privileges should be given to those involved in this program, though those who are not involved should not be made to feel like less of a

Christian for not participating. Not everyone is going to be a leader.

Those involved in this leadership training program should have a personal devotional and prayer diary and should fill out sermon note sheets for the services they attend. The teen leadership meeting would involve a time of sharing what they have learned in their quiet time and in the services during the week. Teens should be encouraged to share what they have learned so they can develop their communication skills, something vital for leaders.

Your leadership meeting should have a prayer time where you pray for each other and for your youth ministry.

There should also be a short teaching time where you teach and discuss a different aspect of leadership each time. Study the various qualities of a leader and look at some biblical leadership roles.

A planning time would involve coordinating and reporting on their various areas of Christian service. Each teen involved in your leadership training program should have a Christian service assignment. As they grow in the Lord and in their leadership abilities they should be given responsibility to oversee an area of the ministry. There are many jobs teens could do which adults are doing. Allowing teens to coordinate and report back on specific areas of responsibility helps them to develop leadership abilities.

The following leadership opportunities can be provided for teens in both a small or large youth ministry:

Small Group Coordinator – this person is assigned a certain number of teens who they keep in touch with and see that they are being discipled.

Communications Network Coordinator – this is

the person other young people contact for information about any aspect of your program.

Transportation System Coordinator – this is the person to call to get transportation to or from an activity. This person secures approved transportation.

Refreshment Coordinator – this person makes sure the right kind and right amount of refreshments are at all activities or whenever needed.

Decoration Coordinator – this person sees things are set-up and decorations are present when needed.

Publicity Coordinator – this person sees that news releases, flyers, and posters are prepared and distributed.

Audiovisual Coordinator – this person sees that the sound system and any audiovisual aids are set up and working properly when needed.

Photography Coordinator – this person sees that pictures are taken at all activities and during other aspects of your program.

Counseling Coordinator – this person makes sure there are counselors ready for the invitation at any function.

Follow-up Coordinator – this person sees that all visitors and decisions are followed up.

As you work with your teens, some will develop leadership abilities faster than others. Be sure you are patient with those who take longer. Also remember you are working with teens, not adults. They may have adult bodies, but they are not adults yet. They are becoming adults. Don't expect more of them than you should. Be sure to let them be teens and enjoy what they are doing.

Though you may involve the teens in various aspects of planning and leading your program, and should allow their input, you should still have planning meetings which are only for your youth workers where the final decisions are made regarding your program.

If you will take practical steps to disciple young people, helping them develop good spiritual habits and leadership abilities, you will see them develop good Christian character in their lives and will see some of them become spiritual leaders for Christ.

CHAPTER FIVE

CHAPTER FIVE
Teaching Young People

Where Does Teaching Fit in Youth Ministry?

Though every aspect of youth ministry teaches young people something, there needs to be some definite purposeful time in your program where your teens, as a group, are taught the Word of God.

Good Bible teaching is one of the most essential elements for a dynamic youth ministry. If your youth ministry merely provides activities which entertain young people, though you may be providing a need in their lives, you are missing the opportunity to have an even greater impact.

God wants us to purposefully teach others the principles from His Word so they can learn to apply those principles to their lives.

"Teaching them to observe all things whatsoever I have commanded you" (Matt. 28:20).

If you will implement an effective means of teaching the Word of God in your youth ministry, you will see the lives of your teens transformed.

"So shall my Word be that goeth forth out of my mouth: it shall not return unto me void, but it shall accomplish that which I please, and it shall prosper in the thing whereto I sent it" (Isa. 55:11).

When Do You Teach?

Some people think the Bible should only be used in church or during Sunday School. They say opening the Bible at a youth activity will turn off teens. My 20 plus years in youth ministry tell me those people are wrong.

I believe the Word of God should be opened at, and be a part of, every facet of your youth ministry. Opening the Word of God is one thing which differentiates us from other youth programs. It helps show how naturally God fits in with everything we do. It also enables us to have an eternal impact on the lives of those present.

I don't mean we need a sermon or in-depth Bible study at every activity. Sometimes only one verse should be read and a brief comment made. Other times a passage of Scripture or some biblical principle should be expounded upon. Other times the purposeful teaching of the Word of God should be the central focus.

Teaching God's Word in a youth ministry can take the form of a devotional, a sermon or a Bible lesson.

1. Devotional – This is a brief presentation of a principle from the Word of God.

Occasion: A devotional is used when people come for some specific non-teaching aspect of your program, such as an activity for your own teens, a meal, a picnic, a game or a work day.

Length: From 3 to 20 minutes in length.

Nature: This usually consists of a lighter topic directly related to the event at which it is used. If unsaved are to be present, a *brief* presentation of the Gospel should be included. This usually does not include an invitation, though an invitation to raise one's hand for prayer may be included.

2. Sermon – This is a clear persuasive presentation of a biblical principle or passage of Scripture.

Occasion: A sermon is used in a traditional part of the program or when the setting allows for it to naturally be used. A sermon is usually part of any service, banquet, retreat, camp, and many activities where both saved and unsaved teens are present.

Length: From 15 to 45 minutes long, depending on the program and effectiveness of the speaker. Twenty minutes is a good average to aim for with teens.

Nature: This is more directive than a devotional and usually involves an invitation to respond. That response could be raising a head or hand, standing to identify a need or coming forward for an altar call.

3. *Lesson* – This is a logical step-by-step presentation which clarifies a biblical principle or passage of Scripture.

Occasion: A lesson is used when it is a natural or central part of the function. Sunday School, leadership training or weekly youth meetings all are appropriate places for a lesson.

Length: From 15 to 45 minutes long.

Nature: The emphasis is on the clear, logical presentation of a topic. This often includes the use of visual aids and some type of student participation or discussion.

Who Should Teach Young People?

In some ways, every youth worker is a teacher. Your life is a textbook your teens read every day. They have an uncanny ability to know when you are real or when you are a hypocrite.

Teaching young people is a serious business. If you desire to purposefully teach young people you should meet the following qualifications:

1. You must have a living, vibrant testimony and personal walk with the Lord.

2. You must be filled with a love for Christ and a concern for teens.

3. You must understand the age-group characteristics of teens.

4. You must understand how to apply the Word of God to their lives and communicate it effectively to others.

5. You must keep abreast of current issues facing young people.

6. You must know how to prayerfully and carefully prepare in advance.

7. You must know how to use teaching aids.

What Do You Teach Teens?

A variety of curriculum and lesson materials are on the market for use in your teen Sunday School and youth meetings. Do not assume a curriculum or lesson material will meet the needs of your young people just because it says it is for teens.

Some curriculum for teens is written by people who have never worked with teens and is not relevant. Some curriculum is doctrinally sound but is practically sound asleep. And some curriculum is so shallow it doesn't have any good doctrinal content.

Whether you purchase a teen curriculum or put together your own teaching materials, you must teach your teens *relevant material in a purposeful way.* Teens need to learn Bible truths in a way they can apply them to their lives. Make sure the material you teach your teens is interesting, practical, and doctrinally sound.

For Sunday School or a weekly youth meeting, teaching a series of topics is often the most effective means of instruction.

For devotionals and sermons it is usually most effective to address stand-alone topics which relate to your teens' daily lives. Review the chapter, *Understanding Young People*, for topic ideas.

If you want to have a lively discussion with your teens, some real good discussion topics are: Abortion, War, Parents, Success, Standards, Careers, Inspiration, Missions, Occult, Drugs, Television, Food, Clothing, and

Teachers. Be sure you study these topics carefully before you have a discussion so you can guide the discussion back to what God's Word says.

Preparing to Teach

Persuasively teaching the Word of God takes preparation. If you will follow these steps you will be able to prepare a devotional, a sermon or a lesson which can transform the lives of your young people.

Begin Your Preparation Early

Don't procrastinate. You need time to prepare to teach effectively. There may be times when you are put on the spot and need to teach without much preparation time, but that is rare. You will usually have advance notice and time to prepare.

Always be ready to teach (2 Tim. 4:2). All youth workers should undertake the following steps and prepare some teachings, even if they do not have a specific time they are to teach. Advance preparation will help you be ready for those unexpected times when you are called upon to teach.

The key to effective teaching is to impart useful information which can be applied to the student's life. Advanced preparation gives you the time to live the teaching yourself. When you have lived what you teach, you will have a much more effective platform from which to teach others.

I had the privilege of working with the S.M.I.T.E. (Student Missionary Intern Training for Evangelism) singers under the direction of Roscoe Brewer for one year. When I was preparing to speak for the team, Roscoe challenged me not to present an intellectual or emotional message but to only teach things I lived in my own life first.

Roscoe said, "A message prepared in the mind affects minds, a message prepared in the hearts affects hearts, but a message prepared in a life affects lives."

That was some of the best advice I ever received. It changed the way I teach and preach and helped make me more effective in ministry.

You may want to use the worksheet at the end of this chapter as a guide for preparing a lesson, a devotional or a sermon.

Step One – Understand Who You Will Be Speaking To

Will you be speaking to all your teens? Or will you be speaking to just the Junior Highers or to just the High Schoolers? Or to just the guys or gals or to both the guys and gals together? Will parents be part of the group you are to address? Will the group consist primarily of saved or unsaved?

Remember each of these groups, or combinations of them, have different needs which need to be addressed differently. Understand both the age group and spiritual characteristics of the group you are to address. In combined groups, address needs which relate to everyone present.

Step Two – Identify the Setting

The occasion can set the spiritual climate of your audience, so you need to understand the climate.

Will you speak for an activity or a regular teaching time? If you speak for a regular teaching time or church service, the teens will expect to hear a sermon or teaching. If you are to speak for an activity, remember the motivation for most of the teens to come was for the activity. They probably didn't come because you were going to speak.

How large a group is expected? Will you and your teaching aids be able to be seen and heard clearly?

When will you speak? Will people anticipate an activity or meal after you speak or will you speak in the middle or at the end of the program?

You need to understand the physical setting. Where will the meeting be held? Will it be held in a church auditorium, in a classroom, on a gym floor or outside? This will affect what teaching aids you can use. For example, slide projectors are not very effective outside during the day.

Where will you speak from? Will you have a pulpit or a stand for your Bible and notes or will you speak without one?

How will the audience be seated? If people are sitting in a circle and you are in the middle, you will not be able to use certain teaching aids.

Will there be a sound system to amplify your voice? If you are outside, sound does not travel well with a large crowd unless you have a sound system.

Step Three – Define Your Goal

A goal takes your purpose and derives a specific measurable statement of what you want to accomplish. A purpose is a general statement such as "to preach the Gospel." A goal is a specific statement such as "to present the Gospel so it can be clearly understood by the teens present at our youth activity, using the Scriptural teaching regarding the Philippian jailer, and giving those present an opportunity to respond with an invitation." That is a specific goal which you can see if you have accomplished.

Sometimes the goal you want to accomplish is stated for you. Stated goals often come from the person in charge of your program, a lesson manual, a book study, a promotional theme, a quarterly topic or a lesson series.

Sometimes you have to decide on a goal by yourself. If you have to determine the goal yourself, do the following:

1. Determine the Needs. Think of the short- and long-term needs of your group. What do they need to know? Draw ideas from the section on influences and issues your teens are facing and from your experience with your teens. Consider talking with other youth leaders for ideas. Share the list you compile with your leader or pastor and ask for additional input. Find other ideas in books or articles relating to youth ministry.

2. List Specific Biblical Principles your teens need to know. Keep this list for future reference.

3. Prayerfully Determine Which Need or Principle to Address. Set forth a goal for presenting the topic you have chosen. Discuss your selection with your leader.

Step Four – Gather Information

Keeping your goal in mind, you need to gather information and ideas to accomplish your goal.

1. List Scripture References That Apply to Your Goal. After you have listed the verses you know, look them up and search for additional references. A good source for Scripture references are:

- Cross references in study Bibles. As you look up verses which apply to your topic, look for references to other verses, noted in the column or at the bottom of the page.

- Concordances. Use this like a dictionary. Look up words which relate to your topic and you will find all the Scripture references where those words are used.

- Topical Bibles or Bible dictionaries. Use these like an encyclopedia. Look up words, persons, places or things which relate to your topic.

- Commentaries. These address passages of Scripture verse by verse. It is good to have a one- or two-volume whole Bible commentary. Look up what the commentator says about passages which address your goal.

2. Next to Each Verse, Briefly Summarize the Principle Which Relates to the Goal. Now that you have compiled a number of verses relating to your goal, carefully determine what biblical principle each one teaches.

3. List the Benefits of Applying the Goal to Their Life. List as many benefits as you can, both short- and long-term. Try to see these from your teens' point of view and from God's point of view.

4. List the Consequences of Not Applying the Goal to Their Life. Do this the same way you did the benefits.

Step Five – Compile Illustrations

Illustrations are often the windows that open doors of understanding. Use illustrations which make the truth come alive. People remember truth which is illustrated more than they remember philosophies and vague or abstract concepts.

Be sure your illustrations are applicable, consistent and understood.

There are four types of illustrations. Jesus, the Master Teacher, used all four:

1. Personal Illustrations. These illustrate the truth by showing how YOU applied it to YOUR life. They carry a high level of credibility. Jesus used this when He told His disciples to love as He loved (John 15:13; 3:16).

2. Second-Hand Illustrations. These relate how the truth you are teaching worked in the life of someone you know, met or read about. Be sure you can substantiate these. Jesus used this when He taught about the Rich Man and Lazarus (Luke 16:19-31).

3. *Scripture Illustrations* – These relate how the truth worked in the life of someone from the Bible. These are very credible. Jesus used this as He spoke of the days of Noah (Matt. 14:36-39).

4. *Symbolic Illustrations* – This is where you use symbols or object lessons to illustrate a truth. Jesus used salt, light and seeds to illustrate biblical truths (Matt. 5:13-16; 13:1-23).

Step Six – Organize Your Outline

Now that you have compiled Scripture, benefits and consequences, and illustrations, all you need to do is organize your material into an outline.

An outline is a means of organizing your information, ideas, and illustrations into a logical order to effectively communicate your goal to your audience.

There are three parts to your outline:

1. *The Introduction* – This is the means of getting your listener's attention and introducing your subject.

Possible Introductions:
* *Introduce yourself.*
* *Comment on the occasion.*
* *Ask a question.*
* *Make a true but startling statement.*
* *State your goal.*
* *Read the Scripture.*

Pointers for Opening Remarks:
* *Be sure your opening remarks lead directly into the message.*

- *Don't give your entire life history or testimony unless it adds credibility to your message or directly relates to the message. Teens are not impressed by long introductions.*
- *Don't make your introduction a message in itself.*
- *Make sure your statistics are 100 percent verifiable.*
- *Don't try to amaze teens with your vast knowledge.*

The Body – This is the main part of your message or teaching. It is comprised of main points, which are logical divisions of thought, and sub-points, which are information and illustrations to support your main points.

There are basically two types of teachings. The type of teaching you use determines how you arrive at the body of your message:

a. *Topical*
- List the main points which set forth your goal.
- Organize these into a logical order.
- List sub-points which support your main points.
- Make each point a statement to relate to your goal.
- Support each statement with Scripture.
- Use one or two illustrations for each point.
- Make the application to daily living for each point.

b. *Textual*
- Divide the text into logical divisions.
- Give each division a heading related to the goal.
- List the sub-points which support your main points.
- Use one or two illustrations for each point.

- Make the application to daily living for each point.

3. *The Conclusion* – This consists of two parts:

- *The Summary* – Where you bring your teaching to a close by summarizing the truths and their application.
- *The Invitation* – Where you provide your listeners with an opportunity to make either a private or public commitment to apply the teaching to their lives.

Step Seven – Determine Your Teaching Aids

Teaching aids are not used very often in devotionals and sermons though they are used extensively in lessons. Proper use of some teaching aids could enhance a devotional or sermon.

Teaching aids are a vehicle to help carry your message to your audience. If you want to be a more effective communicator, learn to use a number of different teaching aids. Then use teaching variety in your presentations.

Make a note on your teaching outline as to where you will use teaching aids.

Be sure to practice in advance with whatever teaching aids you plan to use.

Some good teaching aids to learn to use with teens include:

Overhead Projector	Blackboard
Puppets	Whiteboard
Drama	Chalk Talk
Gospel Illusions	Object Lessons
Video	Slides

How Do You Teach Teens?

Preparing to teach is one thing, teaching is another. Good Bible teaching is comprised of communicating information in a way students can understand it and apply it to their lives.

Good communication skills must be learned and developed. It takes practice to communicate effectively.

The Four Elements for Effective Communication

1. The Message

The message is *what* you want to communicate. This is the information and the application you want to transfer to the student. You must prepare this in advance.

2. The Receiver

The receiver is who you are trying to get the message to, *who* you are trying to communicate *with*. The receiver must be ready to receive the message if the communication is to be effective. If you prepare your message but no one is there to receive it, communication will not take place.

3. The Messenger

The messenger is the one trying to transmit the message. This is *who* is trying to communicate. The way the receiver receives the credibility of the communicator will affect how the message is received. Is the messenger qualified to communicate the message? Is the messenger sincere? Does the messenger genuinely care? Receivers evaluate these questions in their minds. If the receivers perceive that the messenger is not credible, qualified or sincere, the communication will not be effective.

There is a saying, *"What you are speaks so loudly I can't hear what you are saying."* It should be better stated, *"What I perceive you to be speaks so loudly I can't hear what you are saying."*

If the messenger is misunderstood, the communication process is affected. Sometimes teenagers will accept a messenger they should reject and reject a messenger they should accept because of wrong perception.

You must build a rapport and make a positive impression on teens in order to communicate effectively with them.

4. The Method

If the first three elements are not properly functioning, the method you use for communicating will make very little difference. If you do have the first three elements in place, your communication may still fail if you do not use an effective method for communicating.

The method you use must enable you to be heard and understood. It must also keep your teens' attention.

Speak clearly and loud enough to be understood. Maintain eye contact. Look at your teens as you teach them. They don't trust someone who cannot look them in the eye.

Two methods of communication used for teaching young people are lecture and discussion.

Lecture and Discussion

There is a place for lecture and a place for discussion. If you use an all-lecture method, you will not be able to gauge how effectively you are communicating your message. If you use an all-discussion method you will miss imparting some of the information you need to communicate.

Sermons and devotionals are often lecture. Lessons are often a combination of lecture and discussion.

If you have both a teen Sunday School class and a weekly youth meeting with a teaching time, be sure you use a different teaching format for both. Sunday School teaching should provide information through instruction which uses primarily a lecture format. Students would participate by reading Scripture, filling out worksheets and answering questions. For your weekly youth meeting, I recommend that your teaching consist of guided discussion which fosters creative thinking. The topics should be oriented toward issues and contemporary problems.

If you do not have both a teen Sunday School class and a weekly youth meeting with a teaching time, alternate between discussion and lecture in your teaching time. You will find that you communicate your message more effectively.

Leading a Discussion

Many people do not use the discussion method of communication because they have never been taught how to lead a discussion. If you are going to use the discussion method and have a profitable discussion time as part of your teaching program you must learn how to lead a discussion.

Discussions have a tendency to wander from the main thought. Sometimes this is good, sometimes it is not.

If you want to effectively lead a discussion so you can accomplish the goal you set out to achieve, you will need to learn the following principles for guiding a discussion:

1. Study the material you plan to discuss.

2. Put together an outline of your material with the main points being either statements for discussion or thought-provoking questions.

A good flow of questions about a topic or statement would include: *What do you (those present) say? What do other people say?* and *What does God's Word say?*

3. Help your teens learn to distinguish between what we feel or believe and what the Bible says.

4. Differentiate between the interpretation of the Word and application of the Word. The Bible is true. A passage interpreted properly may have more than one application but it will never have contrary meanings. For example, God's Word says we should love one another. That is a truth. How we apply that truth to our lives may be different. That is the application.

5. Learn to listen. Listening will help you understand more about your teens. Don't be the first one to respond to what they say. If you are quiet and listen, others will talk and you will have more effective communication.

6. Be sure you understand what someone else is saying. Don't assume their words mean what you mean. Try to rephrase what they say to be sure you understand them. After someone has responded to a question or made a statement you may say, *"Let me see if I have this correct, what you are saying is..."*

7. Let everyone who wants to talk have an opportunity. Don't let someone dominate the conversation. If someone does tend to dominate the discussion time, you may say, "That's a good thought. Let's see what someone else has to say..."

8. Respect people's viewpoints. Don't belittle someone for what they say. Remember many of the influences on young people have influenced them

contrary to God's Word. Many times a teen is only repeating what they have been taught. When you attack what a person says, you are attacking that person and you decrease your chances of communicating effectively.

9. Though you may lead the discussion, always be sure to establish the Word of God as the final authority. Instead of saying, *"Well I believe..."* or *"The truth is..."* why not say, *"Let's take a look at what God's Word says..."*

If you seek to purposefully teach your teens the Word of God using the principles of effective communication, you will see their lives transformed.

WORKSHEET FOR PREPARING A LESSON, SERMON OR DEVOTIONAL

Occasion_____ Date _____

Who will be addressed?_____

What is the *setting*? _____

Will this be a *devotional*, a *sermon* or a *lesson*?_____

What is your *goal*?_____

_____

_____

List *Scriptures & Biblical Principles* related to your goal:

Scripture   Principle

_____   _____

_____   _____

_____   _____

What will be the *benefits* if the listeners apply this teaching to their lives?

Benefit   Illustration

_____   _____

_____   _____

_____   _____

What will be the *consequences* if the listeners do not apply this teaching to their lives?

Consequence   Illustration

_____   _____

_____   _____

_____   _____

List the *main points* which clearly support your goal:

_____

_____

_____

WORKSHEET FOR PREPARING A LESSON, SERMON OR DEVOTIONAL (Page 2)

Title_____ Main Scripture _____

Introduction (How do you get their attention?):_____

_____

_____

Main Point   1._____

Sub-points
    or
Illustrations
- a. _____
- b. _____
- c. _____

Main Point   2._____

Sub-points
    or
Illustrations
- a. _____
- b. _____
- c. _____

Main Point   3._____

Sub-points
    or
Illustrations
- a. _____
- b. _____
- c. _____

Conclusion

Summary:_____

_____

Invitation: _____

_____

CHAPTER SIX

CHAPTER SIX
The Youth Meeting

What Is the Youth Meeting?

The youth meeting is the heart of a dynamic youth ministry. It is the regular weekly time where your group is drawn together for fun, fellowship, and practical study of God's Word.

The success of your youth meeting does not depend on the size of your youth group. In a small youth group, the youth meeting may only have one worker and two or three teens. That meeting can be as effective as a large youth group which may have upward of 100 plus teens and 10 or more workers. No matter how many teens or workers you have, the youth meeting can and should be a great time for everyone.

Pointers for an Effective Youth Meeting

The youth meeting should be one of the best things you do in your youth ministry. The following pointers will help you have an effective youth meeting:

1. Prayerfully & Carefully Plan.

Our Lord deserves our best. To do a first-class job for Him, you need to prayerfully and carefully plan your youth meetings.

Some people have a hard time planning and getting organized. If you do not plan out the details of your youth meeting it will not accomplish what you want it to. Careful planning helps things go smoothly. If you are not organized, either get organized or get someone on your leadership team who is.

2. Get Your Teens Involved.

The youth meeting is not a time where your teens

come as silent observers. Get them involved in a variety of ways:

Crowd Breakers – Crowd breakers are short, fun activities which break down some of the emotional walls people erect during the week. These are a good fun way to get your teens to open up. A crowd breaker can be an active game which gets everyone to participate or it can be an activity involving a few representatives of the group. On-the-spot scavanger hunts, challenges, surveys and interesting questionnaires make good crowd breakers. Remember not to put visitors or shy teens on the spot with a crowd breaker. Ask for volunteers or use teen leaders who have a sense of humor.

Group Singing – Teens love music. Choose some good songs or choruses that everyone can sing. Singing gives everyone an opportunity to participate. Either print out the words or display them on a board or overhead projector. Make sure you do not violate copyright laws.

Special Music – Using teens for special music provides them with another way to get involved. It also gives them an opportunity for service.

Prayer – Use your teens to pray during your meeting. Use individuals to pray and also pray as a group.

3. Use Variety.

Watch out for the S.O.S. syndrome. Teens bore easily from the Same Old Stuff (S.O.S.). Don't be guilty of adopting the seven last words of the church, *"We never tried it that way before."* Use new ideas and revive old ideas. Don't get caught in a rut.

4. Set Some Basic Rules.

Some basic rules will help your youth meetings go smoothly. If you have rules, make them known but don't sound strict when you present them. Have fun with the rules. Do some skits about them once in a while.

Don't have too many rules. You may want to consider some of the following rules:

- *You must have a good time.*
- *Show respect for others. Listen when someone else is speaking. Don't put others down or make fun of anyone.*
- *No PC. That doesn't mean no personal computers. It means no physical contact. We don't want you sitting around holding hands with guys or gals. If you want to hold someone's hand hold your own. If you want to kiss someone kiss yourself or kiss the youth director's dog.*

If you have a weeknight meeting you may want to add the following rules:

- *Don't drive someone home without their parent's permission.*
- *Don't use tobacco, alcohol or drugs, before, during or after the youth meeting.*

Visitors

Make sure each visitor feels welcomed. During the meeting, teens should be provided the opportunity to introduce their visitors to the group. If a visitor is present and doesn't appear to know anyone in the meeting be sure someone greets him or her, gets to know his or her name, and volunteers to introduce the person to the group.

Be sure you get the name and address of each visitor. That will be very important for follow-up.

Offering

Provide your teens an opportunity to give. Let them

see that their giving is important. Show them how their giving helps minister to people.

Teach them the difference between the *tithe* and an *offering*. The *tithe* should be given to the Lord through the local church. The tithe helps fund the various ministries in the church, including the youth ministry.

The *offering* is above the tithe and is for special projects and nonbudgeted equipment. Select some special projects your teens can give an offering toward.

Testimony or Sharing Time

Testimony time or sharing time helps your teens see how someone has put faith into action. This can have an even greater impact on your teens than your teaching. Truth lived speaks very loudly.

Try to arrange, in advance, to have someone start off this time by sharing either a soulwinning experience, a result from teen visitation, an answer to prayer, a truth they learned and applied this week, or something they learned which they plan to apply in their life.

Be sure the testimonies are to the point. Be ready to tactfully cut someone short who keeps going on and on. Be sure not to drag out this time.

Location

The teen meeting can be held virtually anywhere. It should be a place where teens feel comfortable. It should be a place where they can be active without fear of knocking over something or damaging the place. It should be a place which is easy to find and provides plenty of parking.

The place for your teen meeting should not be too small or too large. The group should fit in the room with a little extra space.

Meeting in the Church

Meeting in the church is ideal for the youth meeting held during Sunday School or one held at the same time as other services at the church.

If your youth meeting is held in the church, have the teacher located near the middle of the longer wall in the room. Set up chairs in concentric half moon rows with a center aisle and two side aisles. Position the sound system operator at the back of the last row. Position the keyboardist near the front where they can see the song leader. Have a registration and literature table near the door.

Sample Room Layout – At Church

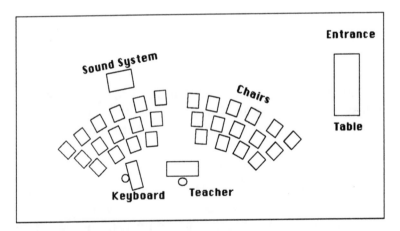

Meeting in a Home

Youth meetings held in a home are conducive to small groups and serve as neutral ground for the unchurched.

You will need a few house rules when you meet in a home. Certain rooms should be off limits. Remind the teens to wipe their feet and to be careful not to spill.

For the seating, try to position the chairs in a circular format. Let the teacher be in the middle near the longest wall. As the group grows, more teens can fit in by sitting on the floor.

The keyboardist, instrumentalist, or tape deck should be located in view of the song leader.

Sample Room Layout - In a Home

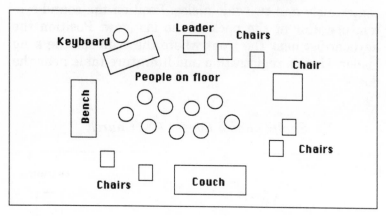

The hosts should not hang around for the meeting, unless they are workers and you want them present. They may help later with the refreshment time.

The Youth Center

If at all possible, designate a room as the youth center. This room would be used for your youth meetings, teen leadership meetings, some activities, and as a fellowship center for the teens. If possible this room should have an outside entrance and exit so it could be used when the rest of the building is not in use. Some churches have converted their old parsonage or the basement, garage or attic of the parsonage into a youth center.

Get some teens together to decorate the youth room. Some items you may want to include in your room are cushions (to sit on the floor), comfortable chairs, couch, tape or compact disk player, small refrigerator, soda or juice machine, video player, computer, table for literature, piano or keyboard, small portable lectern and a library.

Decorations to use include posters of Christian colleges you endorse, good lighting, an announcement bulletin board (with a calendar), a missionary bulletin board (updated regularly), and a thematic bulletin board.

Some supplies you may want to keep on hand in your youth room include Bibles, books, tracks, video games, board games, darts, and magazines.

Convert a Bus

If you have limited space, or if your church rents facilities which are used for other purposes during the week, you can still have your own youth ministry room. In one church where I worked as youth pastor we found an old bus and converted it into a youth center. Converting things is a biblical concept. We had to move the bus each week, so we got one which was in running condition. If you don't need to move your bus, it doesn't need to be in running condition.

In some states, if you take all but two bench seats out of the bus, the vehicle is no longer classified as a bus and you won't need a special bus driver's license to drive it. Remember not to use it to transport more teens than the law allows on the two bench seats.

Most seats are bolted in with nuts extending underneath the bus. To convert the bus you'll need to spray a de-ruster, like WD-40, on the nuts and let them sit a few minutes before you attempt to loosen them. You'll need a good strong wrench and possibly a torch to get them off.

Fill in the holes from the bolts with filler. You may want to spray paint the interior and possibly the exterior of the bus. Put carpet on the floor. Indoor/outdoor carpet works best. In colder climates be sure to put padding underneath the carpet, or the floor will get very cold. Use contact paper or vinyl wallpaper for the walls. Buy some material and have a few of the teens make curtains for the windows. Curtains lined with a dark material will help darken the bus so it can be used for showing films.

If you will meet in the youth bus at night, hook up some lights using extension cords from the main building.

Consider adding two roof vents with fans to help with circulation on warm days. These can be secured from supply houses and are easy to install.

In cold climates be sure to have a way to heat the bus. You could use an electric space heater. One person I know installed a wood stove for heat in a bus.

The Format

There are basically two general types of formats for your youth meeting. If your teen meeting is held during Sunday School it will probably use a different format than if you meet on a weeknight.

The Sunday School Format

This should be a positive motivational and teaching time for your teens. Include enthusiastic singing, fun, fellowship, special music and practical teaching of God's Word. Do not conduct this meeting like a traditional Sunday School class.

The youth director or youth pastor should lead the meeting and involve teens as much as possible.

In a small youth group all your teens would generally be together for this meeting. As your department grows, and you have more workers, it would be best to split the junior and senior high teens into separate groups. The two departments can function together if they have to, but they will be more effective and grow better when they are apart.

Sometimes you may want to divide your group into smaller groups for the teaching time. There will be times when the boys and girls need to be separated in order to address needs particular to them.

The following format works well for the teen meeting held during Sunday School. The times given are an estimate of how much time to allow for each segment. On Sunday morning, where a service usually follows the Sunday School hour, you are under greater time constraints.

1. Presession – *Refreshment & Fellowship Time*

2. Theme Song & Chorus – *(4 Minutes)*

3. Welcome and Opening Prayer – *(3 minutes)*

4. Crowd Breaker – *(5-10 minutes)*

5. Song – *(3 minutes) Lively*

6. Announcements & Introduce Visitors – *(5 minutes)*

7. Song – *(3 minutes) Good spot to teach a new song. Eliminate this song if you need more time.*

8. Testimony Time – *(5-10 minutes)*

9. Special Music – *(4 minutes) Coordinate with Lesson*

10. Lesson – *(20-30 minutes)*

11. Closing Song – *(3 minutes)*

The Weeknight Format

Often the weeknight youth meeting is structured around an organized club program like AWANA, Pro Teens or Word of Life. Such youth programs often suggest a format to follow. If you develop your own program, you will need to develop a pattern to follow for your meetings.

Weeknight programs held in homes should still be organized, but a little more informal than one held in the church. If you have both a teen Sunday morning meeting and a weeknight youth meeting, make sure you use a different format for each.

1. Presession – *Fellowship Time, Games*
2. Theme Song & Chorus – *(4 Minutes)*
3. Welcome and Opening Prayer – *(3 minutes)*
4. Crowd Breaker – *(5-10 minutes)*
5. Two Songs – *(5 minutes) Lively*
6. Announcements & Introduce Visitors – *(5 minutes)*
7. Song – *(3 minutes) Good spot to teach a new song.*
8. Testimony Time – *(5-10 minutes)*
9. Prayer Time – *(5 minutes)*
10. Special Music – *(4 minutes) Coordinate with Lesson*
11. Lesson – *(20-30 minutes)*
12. Closing Song – *(3 minutes)*
13. Refreshments & Fellowship Time – *(20+ minutes)*

Alternate format for weeknight teen meeting, if you have *both* a Sunday morning *and* a weeknight teen meeting:

1. Presession – *Fellowship Time, Games*
2. Song – *(3 Minutes) Lively Song*
3. Welcome and Opening Prayer – *(3 minutes)*
4. Crowd Breaker/Activity – *(15-20 minutes)*
5. Songs – *(5 minutes) Lively*
6. Announcements & Introduce Visitors – *(4 minutes)*

7. Testimony Time – *(5-10 minutes)*

8. Prayer Time – *(5-10 minutes)*

9. Lesson & Discussion Time – *(20-30 minutes)*

10. Closing Song – *(3 minutes)*

11. Refreshments & Fellowship Time – *(20+ minutes)*

Presession

The time immediately preceeding the official start of your youth meeting is called Presession. If your teen meeting starts at 7 p.m., teens and workers will begin to arrive before the time to start. All workers should arrive 30 minutes early for prayer and set-up.

Turn on some music 15-30 minutes before time to start. The music should be playing before the first teen arrives, to help set the mood.

Small Group Dynamics

No matter how large your teen group grows, it can have that close personal touch by utilizing small group dynamics.

Informally assign each teen to a youth worker and to a teen who serves as a *small group coordinator*. It is not necessary to tell the teens they have been assigned to a particular group.

The small group coordinator and youth worker are responsible to observe and encourage the spiritual and social growth of each person in their group. They can accomplish this by doing the following for each member in their group:

1. *Pray for them in personal devotions.*

2. *Keep attendance records.*

3. *Contact them if they are absent.*

4.   *Visit them.*

5.   *Do things with them.*

6.   *Make sure they are discipled.*

7.   *Recognize important events in their life, such as birthdays, promotions, graduations, etc.*

These small groups help develop teen leadership and see that each teen is individually cared for. Each small group coordinator reports on the progress of their group at the teen leadership meetings.

Refreshments & Fellowship

Teens love to eat and like to spend time with each other. This is very important to understand. You can have a better turnout and a more effective teen meeting if you include a refreshment/fellowship time in your meeting.

If you meet on Sunday morning, the refreshment/fellowship time is best during presession. That will help encourage teens to come on time. If you meet on a weeknight, the refreshment/fellowship time usually fits best at the end of the meeting.

Make sure you have plenty of good refreshments and enough time for fellowship with each other.

Use variety in your refreshments. Hot chocolate, juice and doughnuts may make a good standard snack for Sunday morning, but vary it from time to time. Try different types of pastries, juices, and fruit.

For the weeknight meeting, cold beverages and snack foods like potato chips and popcorn are popular with teens. Be sure you use variety. Perhaps they can make gourmet popcorn one night. Nachos and cheese or pizza English muffins are great variety snacks.

Remember teenagers spill frequently when they have refreshments. This is especially true for junior high guys. They are experiencing rapid physical growth and it takes time for their brains to catch up with their bodies. Their lack of coordination is embarassing to them. Sometimes they will reach out for a cup while they are talking, but their brain doesn't realize their arm grew an inch since last week. The hand reaches the cup before the brain realizes it and over the cup goes and out comes the liquid. Make sure you have a supply of paper towels on hand.

Provide enough time for your teens to fellowship during the refreshment time. Don't hang over their shoulders. Teens need socialization time. If they don't get enough socialization time in your meeting, they may get it some other way which is not good for them.

Music & Your Teen Meeting

Teens love music and so does God. God loves music so much he put five song books right in the middle of the Bible. God also made us musical beings. He gave our bodies a rhythm of their own and made them to respond to music.

Music is a tool. It can be used for evil or for good. Learn how to use music as a tool for good. Then use it in your youth meetings.

1. Provide an Enthusiastic Song Leader.

Choose someone who makes you want to sing. Too many dull song leaders have turned kids off to singing.

2. Visualize the Songs.

Get the words of the song in front of the teens so they can read them and sing them as they go along. This is especially helpful to visitors or unchurched teens who do not know the songs. They will feel uncomfortable if everyone else is singing a song they do not know.

Use song sheets, an overhead projector, poster board, blackboard or slides to project the words.

3. *Use a Theme Song.*

Choose one song or chorus as a theme song for the month or for the term. This should be an enthusiastic song. Start the meeting with this song.

4. *Sing Some Lively Songs.*

Use some fun songs that make the teens smile and laugh. If they can't have a good time at church, where can they?

Do some songs standing. Use clapping or other motions for some songs. Don't have them sing juvenile songs with juvenile motions.

5. *Use Instruments.*

Find a good pianist, keyboard player or guitarist to accompany your songs.

Encourage your teens to bring and play their instruments for the program. Have a practice time where instrumentalists can get together to practice the songs they are going to play.

6. *Use Tapes.*

If you cannot find an instrumentalist, there are a number of split-track tapes available today which you can use for your song time. The instruments are on one track and the voices on the other. If you have a stereo cassette player the voice is usually on the right track. By turning down the volume on the right track your group can sing along without the voices on the tape. If you need the voices on the tape, just turn up the right track.

You can even use records of songs sung by your favorite Christian musicians. Just play the tape and have everyone sing along.

Special Music

Encourage your teens to present special music. Youth workers may sing from time to time too. You may want to form some teen singing groups and perhaps a teen choir (though I would not call it that). This will help your teens develop their singing abilities and offer more special music.

Use instrumentalists, as much as possible, for special music. If you use too many accompaniment tracks many teens will not use their instruments for fear they cannot measure up to the professional sound of the sound track.

Consider getting a sound system for your youth ministry. This will be especially helpful for special music. Some people are too soft to be clearly heard, so the sound system helps them be heard more clearly.

You must teach someone how to operate the sound system and teach others how to sing properly with one.

Develop guidelines for your special music. The following guidelines can be a real help.

1. *Special music must be scheduled in advance. Choose a music coordinator who schedules and screens music.*

2. *Anyone doing special music must practice.*

3. *The song chosen must have touched the singer's heart in a special way. The words to a special song must have meaning and must glorify God.*

4. *If possible, the song chosen for the special music should coordinate with the lesson or theme for the youth meeting.*

5. *Consider a dress code for special music. Don't use*

*special music which is poor quality, not prac-
ticed or sounds worldly.   If you do not have special music, consider selecting a song by a Christian musician, that either sets the mood for the
lesson or reinforces the teaching.*

If you carefully and prayerfully plan and conduct
your youth meetings, you will have an enjoyable time
which will have a positive affect on the lives of your
young people.

CHAPTER SEVEN

CHAPTER SEVEN
Youth Activities

What Are Youth Activities?

When someone says, "We are going to have a youth activity," what comes to your mind? Do you picture an essential part of your youth ministry in action or do you see a program designed to baby sit or entertain teens?

Some youth ministries do not include youth activities as part of their program. Some youth ministries have *only* youth activities for their program. Both of these are missing out on ministering to the total teen. Youth activities are an essential element in a dynamic youth ministry. They help you minister more effectively to the total person.

Youth activities are events which take place apart from your regular youth meeting. Some churches have a weekly youth activity, others have only one a month.

There are basically three different types of youth activities: those designed just for your teens, those which are evangelistic in nature, and those conducted by teens for other people.

The Purpose of Youth Activities

Anyone who works with teenagers can tell you that teens have a lot of energy. Youth activities provide a much-needed outlet for that energy.

Some people do not realize the importance of youth activities. They see them as merely entertainment. While activities do provide entertainment for teens, they are much more than that. But even if they were only entertainment, is there anything wrong with good Christian entertainment?

Christians should be able to have fun together. Jesus said He wants us to have joy (John 15:11). If your teens do not have a good time at church, or through your youth ministry, they will find their good times elsewhere. Sometimes those "good times" will not be the good times you would want them to have.

Some people feel the church's role is to address the spiritual needs in the life of its teens. I agree with that, but we must go beyond sober instruction and not neglect the area of youth activities.

God is concerned about the total person: spirit, soul, and body. *"And the very God of peace sanctify you wholly: and I pray God your whole spirit and soul and body be preserved blameless unto the coming of our Lord Jesus Christ"* (1 Thess. 5:23).

The church must address the spiritual, social, and physical needs of its teens. The youth meeting, the discipleship program, and the teen leadership programs primarily focus on the spiritual and social part of the teen's life. If we only provide that we will not minister to the total person. Activities primarily address the physical and social needs while at the same time having spiritual results. They are a crucial part of any ministry which wants to minister to the total person.

Activities take the teaching from the classroom and move it into the classroom of life. Some of the best instruction I have ever received has been in the classroom of life.

Having activities as part of your program produces a variety of benefits. As you conduct teen activities you can see if your teens are applying what you teach them in the rest of your program. Activities also help you identify some needs you must address in the lives of your teens.

Youth activities also provide a point of contact with unsaved or unchurched teens. Those teens are more likely to come to a youth activity than to a church service or youth meeting.

Remember, the purpose of your youth activities is to minister to your teens, not to youth workers.

Sometimes youth workers become guilty of losing their perspective. They plan activities they enjoy, rather than activities their teens enjoy. Many youth workers remember the good times they had when they were teens, a couple of hundred years ago, and are guilty of trying to relive their teen years, instead of ministering effectively to their teens today.

Too often leaders plan activities they enjoy. They see their teens laughing and smiling at the activities and assume the teens enjoy the activity as much as they do. In reality, the teens have accepted the fact that the leaders are going to plan activities they enjoy and the teen must go along and make the best of it.

Activities must be planned with the teens, not the leaders, as the primary focus.

Ingredients for an Effective Youth Activity

God wants everything done decently and in order (1 Cor. 14:40). Remember the admonition of Proverbs 21:31, "The horse is prepared against the day of battle: but safety is of the Lord." This verse teaches us the importance of the combination of preparation and dependence on the Lord. In Bible times a soldier trained with his horse and made preparations for the battle as though the outcome depended entirely on his preparation. As he went to battle, prepared the best he could be, the soldier knew the ultimate outcome would be in the Lord's hands. He trusted God for the results.

The same must be true of you with your youth activities. If you use the following ingredients you will see how they work together to help you prepare and conduct an effective youth activity. You must prepare, then leave the results to God.

1. Planning

One of the key ingredients for an effective youth activity is careful and prayerful planning. Always plan out an activity in advance. There are too many important details you may overlook and not be prepared for if you do not plan in advance.

Workers who have a hard time with details and advanced planning must either develop those strengths or pull in helpers who already have those strengths. If you work at it, you can develop those strengths. Leadership skills are something you develop, not something you are born with.

An activity which is well planned goes smoother and is more relaxed and productive than one which is not carefully planned.

2. Calendar

Check your church master calendar and the calendars for the schools your teens attend to be sure you do not schedule conflicting activities.

Sometimes you may want to schedule events at the same time as those at school as alternatives for those who are not able or do not want to attend a school function such as a dance or prom. Avoid conflicts as much as possible.

Many teens work after school or have part-time jobs and work on a schedule. If you carefully schedule your activities far enough in advance, they will be better able to fit them into their schedule.

3. Balance

A well-rounded youth ministry will have a balance between the three types of youth activities.

Some activities are geared primarily for *Our* teens. The main thrust of other activities is *Outreach* to unsaved or unchurched teens. And other activities allow your teens to minister to *Others*.

For many churches a good balance would be to schedule two *Our* activities for each *Outreach* and *Others* activity.

4. Variety

Be sure to use variety. Don't do the same thing over and over again. If you find an activity your teens enjoy, don't kill it with overuse. Use it only once or twice a year. It is better to leave teens wanting more, than to leave them wanting no more. Remember that teens bore easily.

5. Location

The location or facilities can make or break an activity. You can have an activity anywhere but the activity must be geared to the facilities available.

A place that is too small, not well lit or not the right temperature can negatively affect the activity.

Consider renting a school gymnasium or community building for *Outreach* Activities. Unsaved or unchurched teens are more prone to come to what they view as a "neutral location."

6. Alternate Plans

Always have a Plan B. If you plan an outdoor activity be sure you also have plans for what to do in case the weather prohibits you from meeting outside.

Do not cancel an activity unless the government closes the roads because of dangerous conditions. Many people will have changed their schedules for your activity. If you cancel an activity, the teens will learn they cannot depend on you.

I planned a snow sculpturing activity one time and was almost defeated by the weather. On the day of the activity there was snow on the ground, but it was bitter cold. It was too cold for the snow to pack for snow sculptures. It seemed like a good reason to cancel. Instead of cancelling the activity we got creative and had a snow piling contest and went sledding. Everyone was ready to sit around the fire for hot chocolate when it came time for the devotional.

Sometimes poor weather will not hurt your activity. An outdoor "Grubby O-Lympics" can work just as well on a sunny day as on a rainy one.

7. Set-up & Decorations

Always preview the facility you plan to use for an activity and be sure to set it up in advance.

Have a sign out front to indicate where you are meeting. Set out signs directing people from the main road to the facility.

Put up some welcome signs. Have signs indicating where the rest rooms or other necessary facilities are. Move unnecessary items out of the way.

If you deal with a rented facility which has offensive signs or advertisements posted, bring some banners or sheets to cover them.

A well-decorated room makes people feel welcome and lets them know you thought they were important enough to take the extra effort for them.

8. Equipment

Have all the equipment and supplies you need for your activity on site, set up, and ready before your activity begins.

Determine if you need a sound system and set it up in advance. Equipment set up for playing some background music before and sometimes during the activity is helpful.

Determine how people will be seated. Do you need chairs and tables? Try to seat people so they are as close to the speaker as possible. Teens can sit on the floor if it is not for an extended period of time.

Make sure you have all the supplies on hand that you need for your game time.

9. Refreshments

Teens love to eat, therefore they love refreshments. Almost every activity should have a refreshment time.

Designate a person to coordinate refreshments. There are many ways to handle refreshments. Often the teens sign-up to bring certain items. You must be prepared for the teen who forgets to bring what he or she is supposed to bring.

Make sure you have enough food. Some teens seem to have a bottomless pit for a stomach. Oversee or help serve the refreshments to be sure everyone gets enough before the bottomless pits finish off everything. It is usually best to limit firsts but have enough for seconds.

Find an area to store and prepare refreshments. How will you keep cold things cold and hot things hot? Choose an area and method for serving refreshments. The people responsible for the refreshments must know when and where to set up refreshments and must have a plan for serving.

Some churches offer a snack bar at some of their activities where teens can purchase beverages and snacks. That may be appropriate at some activities but may not be at others.

If your activity requires you to travel a distance and you need to eat along the way, determine what you will do for the meal. If you have to stop for two meals, ask the teens to bring a bag lunch and buy a beverage for one meal. The other meal could be purchased at a fast-food restaurant.

If the teens will need to purchase beverages, a meal or a snack, recommend a specific amount of money for them to bring.

10. *Registration*

Get the name, address, age, school, grade, and phone number of everyone who attends your activities. This is essential for follow-up.

If a teen has a rural route number for an address, ask for a street address or description of where they live.

A registration table near the entrance to the activity is a good place for getting the visitor information and for collecting any fees for the activity.

11. *Cost*

A nominal charge should be collected for many of your activities. The fee will help offset the cost of the activity. It may help pay rent for the facility or provide an honorarium for the speaker. It could also help with the cost of supplies, decorations, flyers, signs, and advertisements.

Try to keep the cost of your youth activities down as much as possible. Part of the cost for your activities should be covered by your youth activities budget.

Budget out all expenses associated with an activity, in advance. This will help you determine what you should charge.

Charge something for your activities, even if it is just one dollar. The funds collected can go to offset the costs of another activity.

Don't be afraid to put on some activities, from time

to time, which may seem to have a high price tag. Some teens spend a lot of money to attend a concert, buy tapes and CDs or rent a video.

12. First Aid & Activity Insurance

Always have a first aid kit on hand for an activity. Know where the closest hospital is in case of an emergency.

Try to have someone on hand who knows first aid. It is advisable for all youth workers to take a first-aid class.

It is also a very good idea to check with your church's insurance coverage and see if your youth activities are covered under their insurance policy. Some companies offer activity insurance. You usually pay an annual premium for the actual number of teens and workers you have. If your youth group grows after the policy is issued all your teens are still covered.

13. Transportation

One real plus for a youth program is to organize a transportation network. Some teens will not have a way to get to your activities without someone providing them a ride.

One of your teens could serve as the transportation system coordinator. Teens would call this contact person who would secure them a ride from a list of approved drivers.

You may want to include a phone number for rides on all promotional literature for your activities and program.

14. Promotion

Use announcements, mailings, flyers, posters, bulletin boards and the media to promote all your activities in advance.

If you are conducting an *Outreach* activity be sure to post flyers and posters around town at the places where unsaved and unchurched teens can see them. Use newspaper ads, if finances are available. The weekly papers with all the local news are usually the best ones to use. Try to take out an ad in the school newspaper, if there is one.

Contact the newspapers and radio and television stations in your area with enthusiasm and ask for guidelines for submitting news releases. Then write news releases for your activities. You can get a lot of free advertising this way.

Be sure you have a sign outside the place where your activity is held announcing the day and time of your activity. Always have a phone number on the sign so people can call for more information.

15. *Program*

You must plan a good program to have a successful youth activity. What your program contains will depend on which of the three types of activities you have scheduled.

Almost every program should allow time for games or an activity, time for music, time for a speaker and time for refreshments and fellowship, usually in that order.

Make sure the program does not drag on and on. If one part starts to drag, move on to the next segment.

Feature a good speaker and good music at an activity. Remember that most people came for the activity, not for the speaker. The speaker must be able to capture and hold their attention, while relating scriptural truths.

16. *Evaluation*

As with every other aspect of your program, you need to evaluate the effectiveness of what you are doing.

After each activity write out a personal evaluation of the activity. Identify what went right and what you could have done better. Have other workers do the same. Discuss the evaluation at your workers meeting. Always seek to improve.

The Three Types of Activities

There are basically three types of activities: *Our* Activities, *Outreach* Activities and *Others* Activities. A good youth ministry will utilize all three types of activities.

Our Activities

The teens in your church need some activities where they can get together as a group and have a good time of fun and fellowship.

Our Activities are aimed at our teens, not at the unsaved or unchurched teen. Though teens would not be prohibited from inviting unchurched friends to an *Our* activity, they would not be encouraged to invite them. The focal point of these activities is not evangelism. If too many unsaved teens are present the focus will turn toward them.

Unsaved or unchurched teens usually do not have the same behavioral standards as your regular teens and therefore require activities planned specifically for them which are structured in a way to avert potential discipline problems. That is where *Outreach* activities come in.

The *Our* Activities are often a little more informal than the other two types of activities.

This type of activity can provide a healthy dating opportunity for your teens.

Some activities which work well for *Our* Activities are: a Destination Unknown, a Mall Hunt, a Video-Game-A-Thon, an All-Nighter, a Skit Night and Pizza Blast.

Outreach Activities

An *Outreach* Activity is a fast-paced social event designed to provide an opportunity for unsaved or unchurched teens to come in contact with your teens and hear the Gospel.

Outreach Activities show that unsaved and unchurched Christians can have a great time and a lot of fun. This provides an excellent contact point.

Outreach activities are major events. These should be first-class happenings. You need to really do a good job with them. Some activities which work well for *Outreach* Activities are: a Super Silly Stunt Spree, a Gym Night, a Barn Night, a Wild Goose Chase, a Grubby-O-Lympics or a Sno-Lympics.

Others Activities

Others Activities are activities conducted by your teens for others. They provide teens with an outlet to use their abilities and energy together in Christian service. This is not the formal Christian service program in your youth ministry. The Christian service program in your youth ministry provides training and regular ministry opportunities for your teens. *Others* Activities are actual activities your teens conduct for others.

Others Activities help turn the attention away from how much fun your teens have, to how much fun they can have doing something for someone else. These activities help to build spiritual backbone in your teens as well as build better relationships between your youth ministry, your church, and your community.

These activities can be as simple as going to sing at an area nursing home to as complex as putting on a mystery dinner for the adults in your church.

Some activities which work well for *Others* Activities are: a Neighborhood Clean-up, an Adult Mystery Dinner, a Film Festival, a Concert or Drama Presentation, Christmas Caroling, Street Meetings or a Children's Activity Night.

Planning a Youth Activity

Anything worth doing is worth planing to do. If you want a successful youth activity you must plan it out prayerfully and carefully in advance. To do that you must learn to use a few planning tools.

1. Planning Calendar

Put together a planning calender on which you list out all activities and the steps necessary to be accomplished as you approach an activity. This is not the master calender which you post for everyone to see. This is for the leaders only.

Prayerfully choose dates for your activities and pencil in the type of activity – *Our, Outreach* or *Other* – you want to do on that date. Don't put down the actual name of an activity yet. Do that after you use the next few tools.

2. Teen Leader's Meeting

This is where you meet with your teens who are leaders. Discuss previous activities. Find out what was good about the activities and what could have been better. Get some ideas you can incorporate into future activities.

Do not plan new activities at this stage. Use this as an information-gathering and brainstorming session.

3. Youth Workers Meeting

This is where you sit down with other youth workers and plan specific activities to put on your Planning Calendar. Don't forget to plan a balanced schedule.

This is where you begin to work out the details for an activity using an activity planning sheet. If you have teen leaders, go back to that meeting with the activity planning sheet and get them involved in some of the planning aspects.

4. Activity Planning Sheet

An activity planning sheet should address all the items necessary to plan out and conduct an effective youth activity. It should list *What* should be done, *Who* should do it, as well as *How* and *When* it should be done. Be sure to list all equipment and supplies needed for an activity.

It is too easy to overlook a small, but important detail if you do not use an activity planning sheet.

Equalizer Games

Next to the message, one of the most important things at any activity is the games or the active part of the activity.

Many youth workers make a tremendous mistake which limits the number of people they reach with their activities and negatively affects the effectiveness of their youth ministry. That great mistake is to plan activities which give an advantage to the athletic teen. Though many teens like sports, there are many who do not. If your activities consist of basketball games, soccer, hockey, volleyball, football or softball, played with normal rules, you will not minister to as many teens as you can.

Your *regular* teen activities should never consist of any activity that favors the athletic, though the activities may challenge the athletic. What you need are activities which use equalizer games and events.

Equalizer games and events are those which remove all the advantage the athletic person has and puts them on the same par as the non-athletic.

Almost any traditional sport can be converted into an equalizer game. Put a sheet over a volleyball net and what advantage is there if you have someone who can spike the ball if they can't see it? Play softball with a foam bat and foam ball and remove forced running and watch the game become equalized.

If you have teens who love playing sports according to traditional rules and with their athletic advantage, then provide opportunities for that in your youth ministry. But those should never be your main activities.

Brainstorm about game ideas with other leaders and you will be surprised how many equalizer game ideas you will come up with.

Youth Rallies

Youth rallies provide opportunities for your teens to get together to have fellowship with other churches. It can be very encouraging for your teens to see other teens who want to live for the Lord. If you have 10 teens in your youth group it can be very exciting to participate in a youth rally where 150 teens are present.

Youth rallies provide an opportunity for larger churches to help smaller churches and an opportunity for smaller churches to pool their resources.

Youth rallies are usually larger versions of *Our* or *Outreach* type activities. Though there should be some preaching or teaching time at a youth rally, that is not its primary function. Youth rallies are primarily activities. Youth conferences provide the concentrated preaching and teaching times.

Youth rallies are usually best conducted with churches in the same fellowship or denomination as yours. You can run into a lot of problems when you try to have youth rallies with churches whose doctrines are different. Many teens will want to date, and some may marry someone they meet at your youth rally. If they are from different types of churches it can cause problems.

You also need to remember that different churches within the same fellowship may have different standards of conduct for their teens. Learn what those standards of conduct are and avoid unnecessary conflicts. For example, if you want to have an activity with a church that does not believe in mixed swimming, it would be inappropriate to plan a waterfront activity where mixed swimming would occur. There are many other activities you can do without creating a conflict.

Ideally, one church or one youth leader should serve as the coordinator for regional or area-wide youth rallies. Participating churches could take turns opening up their facilities and serving as host church for a rally. They could also provide workers to assist in planning and carrying out the youth rallies. Those workers could meet a couple of times a year for planning sessions with the coordinator.

In some areas it is advantageous to have a youth rally once a month. In other areas it may be best to have one every two months. Learn what works best for your area.

A number of the youth rallies with which I have been involved, very successfully incorporated Bible Quizzing into the *Our* type rallies. We allowed each church a quiz team of three members. We used three chapters from the Gospel of John each month and asked who, what, when, and where questions. The questions were a mix of hard and easy. Points were awarded for a correct answer and points were subtracted for a wrong one.

If you use Bible Quizzing make it fun and fast moving. Don't let it drag out. Encourage the teens to cheer for their team. Give something to everyone on the winning quiz team. Relatively inexpensive plaques can be purchased from a trophy wholesaler. Perhaps the winning church could receive a small trophy.

Always have refreshments at your youth rallies. There are a few ways you can provide refreshments.

1. You can assign certain items for each church to bring.

2. You can have the host church provide refreshments.

3. You can charge a fee and provide refreshments.

4. You can offer a snack bar.

Allow adequate time for refreshments and fellowship. Teens need time to get to know teens from other churches. Don't be the last ones to arrive at an activity and the first ones to leave. Give your teens more time for fellowship.

Some activities which work well for youth rallies are concerts, banquets, films, plays, gym nights, a wild goose chase, "Grubby-O-Lympics" and "Sno-Lympics."

Youth Conferences

Youth conferences are similar to youth rallies except the main emphasis in a youth conference is on what they are going to learn. Youth conferences should consist of good teaching or preaching from which teens learn something practical they can apply to their lives.

A youth conference should include a fun time. An activity may be included as part of the conference, but the main emphasis is on what they are going to learn.

Some youth conferences will have separate sessions for boys and girls, some for older and younger teens, and some for youth leaders and youth workers.

Youth conferences usually have a theme which clearly states the goal or purpose of the conference. It may deal with basic things like the Christian walk or with practical topics like "Using Your Talents and Abilities for the Lord." It could be a music, missions, or evangelism conference or one on the Bible and science. There is almost an inexhaustible supply of themes and types of conferences you can sponsor.

If you are unable to conduct a youth conference in your area be sure to take your teens to one somewhere else. These conferences can have a tremendous influence on their lives.

Youth Trips, Retreats & Camps

Youth trips, retreats and camps provide teens with the opportunity to get away for some fun, fellowship, and teaching from the Word of God. These get-aways can have a real impact on the lives of your teens.

Youth trips can be as simple as a day trip to a local park, historic site, recreational facility, sporting event, amusement park or shopping place. They can be an overnight trip to a nearby city, to a youth conference, a camp-out or even a ski trip.

Youth retreats are different than teen trips. They are usually a two- or three-day overnight trip with some type of teaching theme. These can be conducted at a local camp, hotel, someone's home or in the church itself.

Camps are different from trips or retreats. They are usually a time when your teens go away to an overnight facility for five or more days. Either a camp is rented or the group goes to a camp with its own program.

Your teens need some time away from the daily

grind and influences, where you can address specific needs they have as a group. Those times away can create a stronger bond between your teens and workers. It will also provide opportunities to address needs you may never have had the opportunity to address at home.

Your teens also need time away from you and your youth group where they can be with other teens and youth workers who can address other needs in their lives.

I have found that if you or your fellowship conduct your own youth retreat during the year, it is advantageous to select a few good Christian camps and encourage your teens to attend those at another time. If you conduct your own camp, encourage them to also attend another one or to attend a retreat conducted by a camp. You will find the results in their lives can be better than if you are the only exposure to youth ministry they have.

Tips for Traveling with Teens

The following tips are helpful when you travel with teens:

1. Establish a list of policies, procedures and rules before you go. Include such things as where and when they can go apart from the group, and who they need to be with. Include standards for dress and conduct, rules for lights out, etc.

2. Draft some medical releases in case you need emergency medical treatment for any of the teens. Some doctors or hospitals will not even treat a broken arm without such a release.

3. Provide itineraries for teens and parents. List emergency phone numbers for them to call. Have one central number with someone in the church who will serve as a contact person with the group. If you are on the road, check in with the contact person daily.

4. Make sure the teens have a copy of the itinerary, as well as a number to call and rendezvous points in case they get separated from the group.

5. Make a list of what they need to bring. Include everything from shoes to soap. Don't forget to include items like cameras, Bibles, raincoats, umbrellas, flashlights, sleeping wear, and spending money. Consider different lists for guys and girls.

6. List items they should not bring. You may want to prohibit radios and cassette players. Things some teens would listen to will counteract what you are trying to accomplish.

7. Tell everyone to be sure their name is somewhere on everything they bring. Many teens have the same type of items. Name, address, and phone number should be on the outside and inside of all luggage.

8. Be sure your teens have enough money for meals and any other items before you leave. Before you leave, collect money needed for any attractions or places you plan to go that have an entrance fee. Then teach your teens to budget their money so they don't run out the first day or at the first stop. I was on a three-day trip one time where a teen took all the money he had and bought a jacket he wanted at the first stop. He had to scrounge for food money the rest of the trip. That is not right for them to do. With younger teens you may want to bring along a small accordion envelope file to keep their money in and distribute it as needed. Be sure to write down what you give them and have them initial it so it is clear what they have left each time.

9. Plan extra travel time. It always takes longer to get somewhere when you travel with a group.

10. Don't forget to make enough bathroom stops. Some teens have to stop more frequently than others. Be sure everyone understands it will be a few hours be-

tween stops so they will use the facilities, even if they don't feel like it.

11. If teens are on medication, make sure they bring a note from their parents explaining this and explaining what they need to take and how often they need to take it. Assign a person to hold the medication for them. Give the medication back to them each time and have them take their own dosage in front of you so you can be sure they are following the instructions. Do not remove the dosage from the bottle or distribute a medication to any teen unless you are a nurse and are following proper procedures. You could become the subject of a lawsuit.

12. If you travel in more than one car, use CB radios or walkie talkies to communicate with each other. It is too easy to get separated. Arrange for various rendezvous points in case you do get separated.

13. Consider staying in homes or in churches on overnight trips. That is a great way to economize and it can provide a real interesting experience. Be sure guys and girls have separate sleeping and restroom facilities. If possible have the guys and girls in different buildings or at least on different floors.

14. Use vans or consider leasing a travel bus for a long trip. Small cars and school buses are not good for long trips.

Using a Teen Slave Market

A "teen slave market" provides opportunities for teens with limited finances to raise funds for a trip, retreat or camp. It also equalizes the teen who has plenty of money by requiring them to work for part of the cost of the trip.

The teen slave market is often held after a regular service, when the most people are present. Teens are usually sold in four-hour time blocks to do whatever work the buyer has in store for them. The buyer may want the teen to do yard work, help clean out a basement, paint a house, work on a car, baby-sit, do some office work, or just eat their cookies.

Set a minimum bid for each teen. The teens are then auctioned off to the highest bidder. You may want to sell a couple of shy teens as a pair.

Teens who need to earn additional money for the activity may offer themselves for more than one segment.

If you carefully and prayerfully plan out and conduct well-balanced youth activities as part of your youth ministry, using *Our*, *Outreach*, and *Others* activities as well as some youth rallies, youth conferences, trips, retreats and camps, I am sure you will see eternal benefits in the lives of your teens.

CHAPTER EIGHT

CHAPTER EIGHT
Christian Service

God Wants Teens to Serve Him

"For we are His workmanship, created in Christ Jesus unto good works, which God hath before ordained that we should walk in them" (Eph. 2:10).

Every believer, no matter how old they are, was saved to serve. God's desire and plan is for all His children to serve Him. That includes teenagers.

Looking at the opportunities for service in most churches, it seems that some churches think God can only use adults. In most churches there is very little for teens to do in the area of Christian service. Many churches only provide their teens a small part in one of the church services during the annual Youth Sunday.

God sees teens in a different perspective than that. He sees them as believers with the same potential for service as other believers. They can and should have opportunities for regular Christian service. God can use young people.

Throughout the Bible God used young people in service for Him. Everyone knows the story of David, the shepherd boy who became a great king (1 Sam. 16), and the account of Samuel, the young boy who became one of Israel's greatest prophets (1 Sam. 1-3).

In the New Testament there is young Timothy whom Paul exhorted to serve God faithfully, even though he was a youth (1 Tim. 4:1-16).

Many Bible scholars believe some of the 12 disciples were teenagers. Mary, the mother of the Lord, according to the Greek word for virgin, was also a teenager. God does use young people.

Does your church provide a way for young people to be used in Christian service? God wants young people to serve Him. If young people start serving the Lord when they are teenagers, many of them will continue to serve Him when they are adults.

The Benefits of a Christian Service Program

One of the most important things a dynamic youth ministry can do to help their teens grow in the Lord is to involve them in Christian service.

Others activities are one of the ways to get teens started in Christian service. *Others* activities involve the youth group as a whole in ministry to others. These are one-shot opportunities at serving the Lord and provide a good starting point to give your teens a taste of the joy of actively serving God.

After you conduct a few *Others* activities it would be a good idea to start a Christian service program so your teens can have a regular active part in Christian service.

A Christian service program provides opportunities for teens to take their eyes off themselves and channel their energy and efforts into ministering to others on a regular basis.

Christian service gives teens a practical way to take what they have learned in the youth ministry and put it to use.

Christian service can change a teen's perspective on life. It gives them a greater sense of self-worth as they see the Lord using them. It also gives them a sense of importance and the joy of having accomplished something as they see what they can do with God's help.

A Christian service program can help teens see areas in their lives which they need to develop to become more effective servants for Christ. As teens become better servants for Christ, they will also become better Christians and, hence, better people. It will affect their whole life in a positive way.

When I was a student in Bible college, Dr. Jerry Falwell, the chancellor, used to tell us the best thing we could do to grow as a Christian was to serve the Lord. He said it would cause us to take our eyes off ourselves and put them on the Lord. He said it would also cause others to put their eyes on us, which would help us to be more conscious about how we lived our Christian life. I found that advice to be very true and very helpful, both in my life and in the lives of those to whom I have had the opportunity to minister.

Another benefit of a Christian service program is the positive affect it can have on a student's resumé or college or scholarship application. Many colleges look at a student's community service when they have to narrow down the choice of who they can admit. A good Christian service record is a real plus.

Practical Pointers for Christian Service

The following pointers are helpful in instituting a Christian service program.

1. *Provide Opportunities to Serve With Others.*

Many teens need to work with others in ministry before they can minister by themselves. Some will always work better in a ministry where they have to work with others.

Serving with others usually entails opportunities to work within existing ministries in your church. Many programs, like AWANA, provide Leaders in Training programs for the teens. In such a program the teens work as helpers with an adult.

Your teens could help work in Sunday School as assistant teachers. They can serve in the choir or help in the nursery. Teens can serve as ushers or help with the senior citizen or nursing home ministry. They can learn sign language and help in the deaf ministry. Teens can serve as helpers in almost any ministry in the church.

If your church does not have many ministries where your teens can serve, you may want to consider starting a ministry your church does not have.

Some teen groups have a monthly nursing home ministry where they go to an area nursing home to sing and present a service for the residents. You can have teens lead the singing, do special music, read the Scriptures, share testimonies, and even preach. Taking time to visit and pray with the residents can be a blessing to both the resident and the teen.

You may want to start an afternoon Bible club for children or a weeknight Bible club at your church, using teens as leaders. You may want to start a children's sports league where some of your athletes do the coaching. This can be very effective at reaching children who look up to teens who are good players.

There is so much you can do to motivate your teens to serve with other teens.

2. *Keep Friends Together vs. Separate Friends.*

Sometimes it is advantageous to keep friends together to serve the Lord. Two teen basketball or soccer players can be really effective reaching out to others. Two friends who sing together or who know how each other thinks and who work well together can make a tremendous ministry team.

It is even possible to take two friends who always fool around together, find an area of common interest which they can use in Christian service, and channel the enthusiasm they put into fooling around into the Lord's work.

Sometimes you will need to separate friends to get them to develop their potential to serve the Lord. Some friends can never be serious enough to serve the Lord when they are together. Don't walk up to them and tell them you are separating them. Just get them involved in different ministries.

3. Provide Opportunities to Serve as an Individual.

Some teens will not do well serving alone, but many can. God has designed some people to always need to serve with others and others who can do better serving alone.

There will be times in their lives when your teens are going to have to stand alone for God. If they learn to stand alone for Him as a teen, in Christian service, they will be more likely to be able to stand alone for Him later in life.

By serving alone, I do not mean they are off by themselves somewhere doing some ministry, though that may be possible. What I mean by serving alone is they are the one doing the teaching or they are the one doing a solo for special music or they are the speaker at the activity or they coordinate an aspect of the ministry by themselves. Though they will interrelate in their ministry to others, they alone are responsible for some aspect of Christian service.

As you provide teens opportunities to serve with others, watch and see what potential they show for the Lord in specific areas of ministry. Then give them an opportunity to serve the Lord in that area.

Christian service takes many shapes and forms. Remember that serving the Lord does not only mean teaching or singing. Some of your teens will have administrative, organizational or technical abilities which can be used in Christian service.

You and your teens need to understand that the person who tunes up the bus for the youth activity is as important to God as the one who does the preaching at the activity (Col. 3:17). As they do their work unto the Lord, both are involved in Christian service.

4. Provide a Training Program.

Don't give someone a Christian service assignment without training them first. There are too many people placed into Christian service without adequate training.

Training is more than telling someone what to do. Training involves telling them how to do something, then showing them how to do it, then letting them try to do it, then watching them do it, then evaluating what they did and repeating the cycle all over again.

Most people should serve as an assistant or interim before they take on responsibility for an area of ministry.

Your training program must be designed to help them learn how to serve and then improve in their service. It is a good idea to have books, videos and cassette tapes as part of your training program. Attending conferences would be another valuable addition to your training program.

A training program will help identify the strengths and weaknesses of your teens. You may find, in the process of your training program, that a teen would be better suited to serve in another area of ministry. If they want to serve in the ministry they are training for, give them a chance to develop the abilities they need to do it. They should experience joy in serving the Lord.

5. Encourage Them to Do a First-Rate Job for the Lord.

Too many people serve the Lord half-heartedly or in a sloppy or unprepared manner.

Christian service is service for our king and should be done as such. We should give our best to the master. He gave His best for us.

I heard a preacher say one time, "Good, better, best. Never, let it rest, until your good is better and your better is your best."

We need more Christians who will do their best for God. Teens will learn to give their best to God as they see you and other Christians give their best.

Stress the importance of preparation, practice, and self-improvement in Christian service. Though you should be ready to serve the Lord at a moment's notice, there is usually more than a moment for preparation. Again, this is something teens learn from example. How much time do you spend preparing that which you are going to do for God?

Emphasize the need to maintain a close walk with the Lord and the importance of the spirit-filled life. Many Christians get frustrated in Christian service because they depend on their own strength and the flesh, instead of depending on the power of the Holy Spirit.

This truth was so aptly put by George Duffield in the old hymn, "Stand Up for Jesus," when he wrote, "Stand up, stand up for Jesus, stand in His strength alone, the arm of flesh will fail you, you dare not trust your own."

God wants us to do a first-class job for Him. He is willing to help us do it. "I can do all things through Christ which strengtheneth me" (Phil. 4:13).

6. Set Up an Accountability Structure.

One problem we have in many churches is that people are given a responsibility in ministry but are never placed in an accountability structure. There isn't a definite way for them or for others to know if they are doing the job right.

We all need to be accountable to others in our ministries. An accountability structure provides a means for someone to help us know if we are doing what we ought to do.

A weekly Christian service report form is one very good way to help with an accountability structure. Each teen in your Christian service program could be required to fill out a weekly form which indicates what services they attended and what Christian service they performed. They should be encouraged to list a blessing or challenge from their Christian service, plus a prayer request.

A written job description and corresponding standard of performance for their area of Christian service would help each teen know what they are to do and how they are to do it.

You should customize a job description and standard of performance for each teen, before they begin an area of Christian service. Then you should schedule a specific time to review their performance. This will help you and them to evaluate their service. It should identify areas of strengths and areas where improvement is needed. Sometimes you will discover a better area of service for them.

7. *Recognize Faithful Service.*

Some of the least spoken words in Christian circles are, "Thank You" and "You did a good job."

Words of appreciation and recognition mean a lot to people. How many times have you served the Lord faithfully, at great personal expense, and no one seemed to notice. Praise God, He notices. That ought to be sufficient, but it does help when we notice too.

As a youth worker, learn to express appreciation and recognize faithful service, no matter how small it is.

A workers award banquet can be a real blessing. Everyone ought to receive either a certificate or some item of recognition for their service.

Teens really like to get awards or trophies. Giving rewards for faithful service is a biblical principle. God will one day reward us in heaven for our faithful service (1 Cor. 3:8; 1 Tim. 5:18). If God thinks faithful service is important enough to reward in heaven, shouldn't we as leaders think it is important enough to recognize those who serve faithfully on earth?

8.   Consider Establishing a Scholarship Fund.

One great way to encourage faithful Christian service is to establish a scholarship fund. Those who faithfully serve in your Christian service department could earn scholarships for camp or college based on their Christian service.

You can either budget funds for this or encourage contributions to the scholarship fund. You will need clearly expressed standards stating how to qualify and stating the amount of a scholarship for which a student can qualify.

Use a Christian service report form as the record to determine qualifying Christian service. The amount of the scholarship could be based on the number of semesters of Christian service a teen has put in at your church.

Some Specific Areas of Christian Service

There are many ways your teens can serve the Lord. The following are some areas of service which have worked effectively for teens in a number of churches.

Teen Leaders

This area of service was addressed in the section on *Developing Leadership Qualities in Teens,* in chapter four of this book.

Providing teens opportunities to serve the Lord in leadership can help them develop leadership abilities or at least learn how to understand and appreciate leadership better.

Not all of your teens will work well in leadership positions. Don't confuse a teen with an extroverted personality as a leader and an introverted personality as a follower. Some extroverts make poor leaders and some introverts make excellent leaders. If a teen shows an interest or potential in leadership, give him or her a try. All that some teens need is a leader who will give them a chance. With that chance they may be able to develop into a great leader for the Lord.

Teen Counselors

Teens need to be trained to lead other teens to the Lord. They need to know how to do this personally and during an activity. Teens can be more effective at leading other teens to the Lord.

Provide a class or a one-on-one instruction time where you teach teens who are interested in being counselors how to do it.

Include such topics as how to lead a soul to Christ, how to counsel at an invitation, how to deal with sin problems, how to help a person grow in the Lord, how to know when to refer someone to someone else for counseling, and what procedures to follow when counseling.

Teen counselors should be ready to counsel at any activity or service the church has.

Some of your teens are able to learn to do more in-depth counseling. Provide them with reading materials and further training to help them.

Remember it is always best to have your teens only counsel those of the same sex.

Audiovisual Ministry

In this modern multimedia world in which we live, teens are often more familiar with the cutting edge of technology than adults. Many teens will show an interest in new technology and in the area of audiovisuals, an area which can enhance almost any ministry.

Consider training some of your teens to either work in or help head-up an audiovisual ministry. They can run the sound system and coordinate an audiotape and videotape ministry. This is a very practical area of service.

They could help set up and run the sound system for all teen activities and may even help with other services in the church.

Teens could set up a tape ministry, record the messages or Sunday School classes or other special events, then make tapes available for those who missed a session. Remember not to record music in violation of copyright laws.

Your teens could also set up a video ministry which has endless possibilities. They could also establish a videotape lending library.

The audiovisual ministry could also include other equipment like slide projectors, video projectors, special lighting for drama presentations, and more.

Music Ministry

Most teens love music. Music plays an important role in the lives of teenagers. It can be an excellent tool for Christian service.

Music is one of the areas where you could involve your largest number of teens in Christian service. Teens should be encouraged to sing and play instruments for the Lord.

Most teens can sing. They just have to be encouraged and shown how to sing. Consider providing a way to help develop and improve the musical abilities of your teens. If you have a teen choir or teen singing group you should always allow some time during your practices to teach them musical principles and help them improve.

You may need to work with some teens individually to help them develop their musical abilities.

Especially encourage those who have developed their musical abilities to use them for the Lord. As teens see others using their musical abilities for the Lord, they are encouraged to do the same.

One way you can get your teens involved in music as a group is to do a teen musical or musical drama presentation. Simple two-part harmony programs written for teen groups are available as well as more challenging five-part programs.

Teen Visitation

Teen visitation is a great way to get teens involved in sharing their faith with others.

Teen visitation can be conducted on the regular visitation night of the church. Teens could be paired up with an adult or with another teen and would visit teens.

Who should you visit? First, you ought to visit every teen who visits any aspect of your church or youth ministry. These are some of the best prospects to visit. Some of them are already saved but will appreciate the interest you show by visiting them. Some of them will not be saved and you may have an opportunity to share the Gospel on your visit.

You should also visit those who have been absent from your program. Lots of things happen in teens' lives between meetings. Don't let anyone slip through the cracks. Visit the absentees.

Visit your regulars at least once a semester. Going to their homes shows you care. You can learn a lot about your teens by visiting in their homes. It can also provide you with opportunities to establish relationships and to minister to other members in the family.

Finally you should visit prospects. Have teens visit classmates or teens they know. You may want to conduct a survey in your church and see if there are teens who attend some aspect of the church program but do not attend your youth ministry. You may also want to find out who has teenage relatives who do not attend the church. These are good sources of people to visit.

Everyone who wants to go on teen visitation should be required to go through a training program. At first you should take one teen with you and teach them what to say when they visit. Make up a list of what they should know and go through it in a few weeks. When they are ready, let them bring someone else along to train. Then pair off and you take on a new teen to train. After a while you will have a number of teens involved in visitation. Make teen visitation something which is a privilege to attend.

Some churches conduct teen visitation every week and others do it once a month. Do what works best for you.

Outreach Teams

Every youth ministry should consider forming out-reach teams as part of their Christian service program.

An outreach team is a team which is formed to take the Gospel beyond the walls of the church. This could entail going out into the community or going to other churches and beyond.

Practical Pointers for Outreach Teams

1.   *Have a Clearly Stated Purpose for Each Team.*

Don't just form a team for the sake of having a team. Set a specific purpose you intend to accomplish. Sometimes the name of the team will reflect that.

2.   *Have Standards for Team Members.*

Any teen who wants to be part of the team must understand there are certain standards they must adhere to. You should write out a Standard of Conduct. This would address things like church attendance, personal devotions, and correct behavior. You may want to require that they maintain good grades in school. Good grades for one student may be an A and for another it may be a C. You do not want participation in the team to cause their grades to go down. Teens have a tendency, like adults, to do what they enjoy doing and neglect what they do not enjoy. If you give them an opportunity to neglect their studies, some will.

You may want to allow teens to serve on only one outreach team at a time. There may be cases where someone serves on two teams, but be sure not to spread them too thin.

Establish a dress code for your teams. Your dress code should address what they should wear and perhaps what they should not wear when they are traveling and when they are ministering.

3. Develop an Esprit de' Corps for Your Outreach Teams.

Each team should have its own name, and perhaps even its own logo, jacket or some other means of identification. Teens like to belong to and identify with a group which is doing something they like to do.

You could have some special items custom made for your team or you may want to choose some type of standard clothing or colors to identify your team.

4. Beware of Elitism.

Although the teens on a team should have team spirit and be glad to be part of the group, don't let them develop the attitude that they are better than any other teen or team.

Though it is important to serve the Lord, teens must realize serving God does not make them better than anyone else. They are still sinners saved by grace, who only serve by the grace of God.

5. Have Try-outs for Your Teams.

Even if you have a small youth group, and will probably have all your teens on your team, have try-outs for your team. It gives teens a sense of accomplishment to have made it onto a team.

If you have a larger youth group and can only have a few teens on your team, you will definitely want try-outs. Remember the try outs should determine both ability and spirituality.

Let the teens know there is nothing wrong if they are not chosen for a team. Let them know you are looking for the teens God wants on the team.

Some teens who are good soloists may not have a voice that blends well in a music group.

6. Don't Let Your Teams Be Your Only Christian Service.

Some teens may not make it on a team, but they need a place of service. Outreach teams usually center on evangelism, which is only one aspect of the Great Commission. Teens need opportunities to be involved in many aspects of Christian service.

7. Have an Adult Coordinator for Each Team.

Each team should have its own adult coordinator. The adults will help their teams in any way they can. They should be spiritual leaders as well as people with an interest and preferably abilities in the area of their team's speciality.

The adult coordinator should work with the team leader to help the team accomplish its purpose and become all the Lord wants it to be.

8. Have a Team Leader.

The teen team leader should be a spiritually mature teen. This provides a great opportunity to develop Christian leadership.

The teen team leader should work closely with the adult coordinator. This person should help set the spiritual tone for the team and should be able to provide some direction for the team. This person should have abilities in the team's speciality and should be prepared to speak for the team.

9. Have Prayer & Practice Times for Your Teams.

If you have a teen leadership meeting the same night as your church's midweek service, that would be a good night for your outreach team meetings. You could have your teen leadership meeting first, then allow segments for your outreach teams.

Every team needs a time to pray and practice together, no matter how well they know what they are doing.

10. Have Scheduling Policies.

You need to determine specific policies as to where and when your teams will go out to minister. If your teams do a good job, they will be in demand.

Will they go to other churches, to camps, retreats, and banquets? If they go out on the street should they go to parks, beaches, street corners, and shopping malls?

What if another organization asks them to come? Where would you go and where would you not go? How far away will you travel?

Remember the other activities and commitments in your teens' lives. Don't overschedule but don't underschedule them either.

Who does the scheduling? Who do they contact? The team leader should be allowed to make some calls to schedule the team but the final approval should come from the adult coordinator, who checks with the youth leader and master planning calendar.

11. Have Financial Policies for Your Teams.

Outreach teams incur expenses. Besides office expenses and materials, there are traveling and promotional expenses. You should budget some money for this, but it will often not be enough. Determine if the teens need to purchase some of their own supplies.

Opportunities may arise for the teams to receive an offering and honorarium. Determine if you are going to ask for traveling expenses when your team does something for another group. Other churches or organizations who ask you to come should pay your traveling expenses and provide meals and lodging in addition to taking a "love offering" or giving you an honorarium.

If you contact another church as an outreach project, you may want to only ask to receive a love offering to help support the work of the team.

Determine what you will do about meals as you travel. It is a good idea to have your team pack the first meal. You can ask a host church to pack a meal for you to eat on the way home. That reduces expenses considerably.

Each team should have a budget they follow, just like the rest of the youth program. An approval policy should exist for all expenses, before they are made, along with a means for allocating funds.

12. *Have Promotional Packets for Your Teams.*

If you take the effort to put together an outreach team you should take the extra effort to put together a promotional packet.

A promotional packet should contain news releases about the team as well as flyers and posters. This could be a simple basic packet or one which is very elaborate. Have your teams help prepare these promotional packets.

The promotional packets can be used to make people aware of what your team is doing. Newspapers are always looking for religious news. Before you go into an area, send the newspapers a news release.

The packets will also help a church promote your team so there will be more people present when you minister.

Flyers are very helpful, even if you are doing park or street meeting. You can pass out flyers and tell people when and where your team will be doing what they do.

You may also want to make up some signs for your team. It would help to have a sign outside the building or location where you are ministering, so people know ple know something special is happening. Also place a poster inside of the building as people enter the room where you are ministering. An attractive banner would also be nice for the room in which you are ministering. Be sure to make your signs and banners durable. They will take a lot of wear and tear.

Types of Outreach Teams

There are many different types of outreach teams you could form, depending on the interest and abilities your teens have.

1. Music Team

Put together one or more groups from your youth group who sing or play instruments together. Select vocalists, instrumentalists, a speaker, and a sound system operator.

2. Drama Team

You can either write your own or purchase some Christian skits and plays to perform as a group.

Choose a director, writers, actors, stage hands, costume designers, make-up personnel, prop & stage builders, lighting personnel, musicians, ushers, and sound system operators.

3. Puppet Team

Many different types of puppets are available and there are many different ways to use puppets. You can have an all-puppet program or a combination of people characters and puppets.

This team needs puppeteers, writers, voices for puppets, puppet and costume makers, stage makers, stage hands, and sound system operators.

4. Open-Air Evangelism

There are many different versions of open-air evangelism teams. Usually you have someone to get the crowd's attention. This can be a musician, puppeteer, a chalk artist, a flannelgraph storyteller, a juggler, a Gospel illusionist, a clown, a mime or anyone else who can draw people's attention.

Then you need someone who can present a clear Gospel message. It could be any of the above mentioned people or someone else.

You also need people to deal one-on-one with those who gather around and with those who may start to walk away.

5. Sports Team

A sports team could be two or more athletes in your youth group who excel in a particular sport. They can use their abilities in open-air evangelism to draw a crowd, on the basketball court or wherever there are people. They are also effective at youth rallies, camps, and retreats.

Almost any sport can be used: basketball, soccer, karate, judo, weight lifting, tennis, and so on.

6. Bible Club Team

This team conducts neighborhood Bible clubs or vacation Bible schools in churches or in the community.

You need someone who can lead singing and someone who can teach. You may also want someone who can direct games and lead a craft time.

Missions Exposure

One of the most beneficial spiritual experiences a teen can have is to be involved in a missions exposure trip. Participating in such a program will help teens better understand missions. It can help them understand if they should either go as a missionary or faithfully support those who do go.

There are a number of ways for teens to get involved in missions exposure trips. Many youth organizations, like Word of Life, have exposure trips for teens each year.

Normally a teen applies for a program, based on a recommendation from their home church, then raises support for the trip. Usually the home church helps with a significant portion of the trip or has a scholarship fund for any teens who participate in missions exposure trips.

The length of an exposure trip varies. It can be as short as a weekend to as long as an entire summer. It can be done almost any time of year. Some groups go during the summer, some go during other school breaks.

Some youth groups try to get a whole group of their teens to go together on such a trip. Some organizations, like Challenge International Missions can help you plan such a trip. There are many details to attend to, like travel arrangements, passports, visas, shots, travel insurance, transportation, lodging, meals, and more.

Many of the missionaries your church supports would love for your teens to come for a visit.

There are various things your teens can do on a missions exposure trip. Sometimes they can help with children's meetings or evangelistic crusades. Sometimes they can be involved in street meetings and tract distribution. Some groups go to a field to help with manual labor on a work project. Sometimes it is just a "go and watch" experience.

If you are going to a country where they do not speak your language, get some cassette tapes of the language so your teens can learn some words before they go. It would be a real blessing if your teens could learn some songs in the other language.

Christian service is a very important aspect of a dynamic youth ministry. As you implement a Christian service program in your youth group you will see them grow closer to the Lord and closer to each other. The program is certainly worth the time and effort.

APPENDIX ONE

APPENDIX ONE
Teaching Topics

Many youth workers are constantly on the lookout for teaching materials to use in their youth programs. A number of publishers and youth organizations publish curricula and teaching materials for youth.

This section contains some suggested teaching topics you may want to use in your youth program. These topics may be used for your Sunday or weeknight teen meetings. Besides serving as good lesson topics they could also be used for discussion topics or devotionals.

Four Different Types of Series

A 10-week series of lessons seems to work well. There are four distinct types of series which you should seek to use throughout the year. Two doctrinal series and one of each of the others could provide variety and balance to your teaching.

1. Doctrinal Instruction Series.

These studies provide foundational instruction in biblical truths. Teens need a solid doctrinal foundation to build their lives upon. Pure doctrinal instruction by itself is not enough.

2. Personal Instruction Series.

These studies deal with issues which teens face as individuals in their personal life and in their walk with God.

3. Relationship Series.

These studies deal with relationships with other people. Every day teens have to deal with other people. God's Word is full of handles to help us in those relationships.

4. Christian Service.

These studies deal with topics which focus on serving the living God. Teens need practical instruction in how to serve God.

Sample Youth Series Topics

If you put prayer and careful study into these sample topics you can develop a lesson plan that will minister effectively to your teens.

Doctrinal Instruction Series

1. Discovering Hidden Treasure.

Objective: To stimulate a hunger for the Word of God in the students' lives. This series will show the student that the Bible contains much more than just names, dates, and places which sometimes seem like ancient history. The student will see that the Bible is filled with romance, action, adventure, humor, and a lot of practical advice which works.

Lesson Topics:

1. You Must Look to Find Hidden Treasure (Prov. 2:1-5)

2. Interesting Scientific Facts in the Bible

3. Explanations for the Unexplainable: Sea Monsters, Atlantis, Dinosaurs, Ghosts, etc.

4. Romance: Samson and the Song of Solomon

5. Humor: Elijah on Mt. Carmel, Baalim, Peter & Rhoda

6. Action & Adventure: David & Saul, Jehu

7. The Supernatural: God's E.T.s, Demons & Angels (John 5:4; 2 Kings 6:8-17)

8. Intrigue: Esther & Haman

9. Practical Advice Which Works (Proverbs)

10. The Formula for the Happys (Psalm 1)

2. *Difficult Questions.*

Objective: To help students see that God's Word contains answers or principles which can answer even the most difficult questions.

Lesson Topics:

1. Where Did Everything Come From?

2. Why Did God Make Hell?

3. What Is Heaven Like?

4. Why Are There So Many Different Churches?

5. Why Does God Allow Evil?   Why Do Bad Things Happen to Good People?

6. How Did People Get All Over the World and Why Do They Look So Different?

7. Why Doesn't God Save Everyone?

8. How Does God Talk to People?

9. Do Christians Worship Three Gods?

10. What Is the Sin Unto Death?

3. *Truths You Can See.*

Objective: To help students see how to make personal application from object lessons and parables in the Bible. Students will see how biblical principles can be learned and illustrated with simple objects around them.

Topics:

1. What are Parables? (Matt. 13:10)

2. Light (Matt. 5:14-16; John 8:12)

3. Salt (Matt. 5:13; Col. 4:6)

4.   Water (John 4:5-15; 7:38)

5.   Seed & Ground (Luke 8:4-15)

6.   Sheep (Isa. 53:6; Matt. 18:12-14)

7.   Coins (Matt. 22:15-22)

8.   Yeast/Leaven (Matt. 13:33; 16:6)

9.   Doors (John 10:1-18; Rev. 3:20)

10. Object Lessons You Can Use: Flashlight, Vinegar, Coal

4. *Understanding What Other People Believe.*

Objective: Many people sincerely hold to varying systems of beliefs. Students need to see what those systems involve. They need to understand how beliefs affect people's lives so they can gain a better understanding of how to effectively witness to others.

Topics:

1.   Why Man Has Religion

2.   Judaism

3.   Catholicism

4.   Protestantism

5.   Sects

6.   Cults: Part One

7.   Cults: Part Two

8.   Islam

9.   Far Eastern Religions

10. Secular Religions

Personal Instruction Series

1. How to Succeed in Life.

Objective: To provide students with practical principles from the Word of God to help them succeed in life.

Lesson Topics:

1. Good Success and Happiness (Josh. 1:8; Ps. 1)
2. Understanding the Conflict between the Spirit and the Flesh (Gal. 5:16-26)
3. The Battle for the Mind (2 Cor. 10:3-5; Phil. 4:8)
4. Adding to Your Faith (1 Peter 2:5-7)
5. Resurrection Living (Rom. 6:1-10)
6. Personal Finances (2 Cor. 8-9)
7. Setting a Course (2 Tim. 4:7; Acts 20:24)
8. Controlling Your Time (Eph. 5:16-17)
9. Applying the Replacement Principle (Isa. 1:16-17)
10. Getting Good Counsel & Being Accountable to Someone (Ps. 1; Prov. 1:20-33; 8:1-21).

2. Dealing with Difficult Situations.

Objective: To help students learn to deal with difficult situations they may have to face in their personal lives by applying biblical principles.

Topics:

1. What to Do When It Seems Everything Is Going Wrong
2. Moving to a New Area
3. Dealing with Death: Loves Ones and Friends

4. Surviving Separation or Divorce

5. Dealing with Disease: AIDS, Cancer, etc.

6. Drugs and Substance Abuse

7. Suicide

8. Premarital Sex and Pregnancy

9. Dealing with Abuse

10. Dealing with Betrayal and Persecution

Relationship Series

1. *Making Life's Choices.*

Objective: To prepare students to make the right choices in life by providing practical principles from the Word of God which can be used when they must face choices involving other people, which affect their lives.

Lesson Topics:

1. Right, Wrong, and In-Between?

2. Christian Liberty

3. What Standards to Use for Making Decisions, Where Do You Draw the Line?

4. Separation and the Replacement Principle

5. Preparing in Advance

6. When It's Cool Not to Be Cool

7. Culture, Music and Entertainment

8. What about Clothing?

9. Alcohol, Cigarettes, Drugs, and Food

10. Friends and Dating Standards

2. *Dating Can Be Great.*

Objective: To help students understand the purpose

for dating and to help them develop guidelines which will make dating productive and fun.

Topics:

1. Cultural Considerations
2. Sexual Awareness
3. What Is Courtship?
4. Types of Dates
5. Going Steady
6. Engagement
7. Questions to Ask
8. Marriage
9. Don't Forget the Future In-Laws
10. Developing Guidelines

Christian Service Series

1. You and Your Church.

Objective: To show students the dynamic role their local church can play in their lives. They will learn about ways to use their talents and gifts to minister in and through the church, in a way that makes a difference for eternity.

Topics:

1. What Is the Church (Matt. 16:18)?
2. The Purpose of the Church (Eph. 4, Heb. 10)
3. No Perfect Churches: A Look at Some New Testament Churches
4. Serving the One Who Gave Everything for You
5. God Wants to Use You: Understanding the Gifts, Part One (1 Cor. 12:1-6)

6. God Wants to Use You: Understanding the Gifts, Part Two (Rom. 12:1-8)

7. Finding Your Place of Service: Understanding the Different Ministries

8. Doing Something That Counts: Greater Works (John 14:12)

9. Becoming a Follower and a Leader (Matt. 20:20-28)

10. Resolving Conflicts in the Church, God's Way (Matt. 5:23-24; 18:15-20)

2. *Sharing Your Faith.*

Objective: To help students understand what a wonderful gift eternal life is and to equip them to share that gift with others.

Topics:

1. What Is Faith and Salvation?

2. Salvation Terms

3. Personal Evangelism (John 15:1-16)

4. Leading a Soul to Christ: Part One

5. Leading a Soul to Christ: Part Two

6. Visitation

7. Counseling at an Invitation or Activity

8. Open-Air Evangelism

9. Creative Evangelism

10. Follow-Up

APPENDIX TWO

APPENDIX TWO

APPENDIX TWO
Youth Activities

Youth workers are always looking for good ideas for youth activities. Variety is a key to an effective activity program. You need a mix of the familiar and the new.

One of the best ways to get ideas for activities is to talk with other youth workers, then spend some time brainstorming with your workers and teen leaders.

Don't be afraid to try something new or revive something old. Remember the important thing is for the activity to be fun for all involved.

Make sure you don't get caught up in the bigger-and-better syndrome. Some youth workers keep trying to outdo themselves with each activity. This is often due to an improper perspective on youth activities. If you have a balanced program, with teaching, activities, and Christian service, and use a balance of *Our*, *Outreach* and *Others* activities – you will not have to keep doing bigger and better.

Remember, you do not build your youth ministry on activities, you build it by building your teens and teaching them how to reach their friends.

The following ideas will help you get started on some activities. Take these ideas and expand or modify them in your planning sessions.

"Our" Activities

1. *Destination Unknown.*

Teens meet at a predetermined location and go together to an undisclosed final destination. The final destination could be someone's home, another church, a restaurant, a park or some other special place.

Don't go directly there. Make getting there part of
the fun. One time we blindfolded the teens and drove
around a few blocks and led them in the back door of the
church to a room decorated in a different manner. None
of the teens knew where they were when they were un-
blindfolded.

You can do a variety of things at your destination.
You can have a low-keyed get together at someone's
house or an action-filled activity.

One time I took a group of teens from Connecticut on
a Destination Unknown. All they knew was we were going to get ice cream and we were going to be home late.
Our final destination, unknown to them, was Times
Square in New York City.

2. *Graduation Banquet.*

This is used sometimes as an alternative to the high
school prom. If you have a large youth group you can either rent a facility or have a catered affair. If you have a
small group, make reservations at a nice restaurant and
plan a nice evening together for the graduates.

In small youth groups often the whole high school
teen group is invited to the banquet and the graduates
are the guests of honor.

In one youth group we only had two seniors, so we
took them to an exclusive Japanese restaurant with a
beautiful flower garden you could walk through before
or after your meal. It was a dress-up affair. They each
brought a date and had a very special evening.

3. *All-Nighter.*

Plan a whole evening of activities ending the next
morning. You may want to plan the early evening at
some other location and return to the church or someone's house around midnight for the rest of the activities.

Some possible activities to include in an all-nighter could include: attending a sporting event, going to a mall for an hour or two of shopping, watching videos, going roller skating or bowling, playing board or video games, going to a gym for some games, eating out, praying together, etc.

Remember to have your devotional early on in the evening. Some teens and even your speaker may fall asleep if you try to have devotions at 2 a.m.

It takes a lot of refreshments for an all-nighter. Be sure to have some pillows and blankets along for those who want to curl up in the corner and catch a few winks.

4. Bicycle Trip.

You could take a simple five-mile bicycle trip or a more extensive 20-50 mile cycling trip. If you are taking a longer trip, tell your teens to practice cycling in advance.

Be sure to have some bicycle repair tools along for a longer trip. Some bicycles will break down.

My older brother went as a mechanic one time on a teen bicycle trip from New York to Florida. You could take a long trip for a weekend or for a week. You could arrange for lodging in churches along the way and even participate in a service or two.

5. Take a Hike.

Take the group for a hike in a park, out in the desert or up on a mountain. Be sure people know how difficult the hike will be in advance.

If you go for a hike in the mountains it is usually best to have three or four groups. Each group could take different routes according to their abilities.

Sometimes a hike can be more interesting if you

have either a nature scavenger hunt or a nature photo hunt along the way, using Polaroid™ cameras. Each group can try to get a picture of certain items or of the group at certain types of places.

6.   *Everyone's Birthday Party.*

Consider having a big birthday party for everyone at once. Everyone could draw names of someone to buy a present for.

You can have a big cook-out and a large cake. You could go to a park or to an amusement facility for the day and have a great time together.

7.   *Video-Game-A-Thon.*

Set up a number of video games at one location and have your group play a variety of games for the night. Have prizes for the highest score. It is a good idea to provide some board games and games like darts and Ping-Pong as alternatives. Set a time limit on board games.

This can be used effectively with a youth rally. Each church tries to accumulate as many points as they can during the evening.

8.   *Skit Night and Pizza Blast.*

Divide your teens into teams in advance and have them prepare a variety of skits. This works great with a youth rally with other churches. Have an all-you-can-eat pizza blast as part of this activity, or use whatever food your teens like best. Be sure to have lots of beverages on hand for this one.

9.   *Video Camera or Cassette Scavenger Hunt.*

Provide each team with a cassette recorder or video camera and have them go on a hunt to try to capture certain images or sounds on tape.

You can do this as a silly activity or a very serious one. For the silly activity, make a list of sights or sounds which they must try to record. The sillier the item the more points it is worth. Some suggested things to find are: a cow mooing, a dog barking, a cat meowing, a rooster crowing, a fire engine sounding its horn, a policeman blowing a whistle, a baby crying, children singing "Jesus Loves Me," men singing "Jingle Bells," etc.

For a serious activity each group could be assigned a series of questions to ask strangers to answer. They could ask around the neighborhood or mall. Some questions could be: If you could have one wish, what would you wish for? What is the most important need in the world? How can someone get to heaven?

10. Bigger and Better.

This is an unusual activity which can be a slow starter but then really gets moving fast as it goes on.

The teens are broken up into groups, given some small item like a bottle of shampoo, and are sent out into the surrounding area. They are to go door to door and tell people where they are from and that they are on an activity called, "Bigger & Better." You may want to print flyers which they can hand the people they talk with.

Each group explains to the people that they are to try to find something bigger and better than what they have with them. All items received will either be used in the ministry or donated to a mission or homeless shelter.

You will be amazed what people will give and what your teens will come back with. I have known of groups to come back with lamps, lawn mowers, stereos, and even a car.

This is a great activity to break down the fears of going door to door, something which will help the teens in evangelism later. It really helps to have at least one extrovert on each team.

Outreach Activities

Some of these *Outreach* activities can also be used for *Our* activities. These are effective activities for your teens to invite their unsaved or unchurched friends to.

1. Super Silly Stunt Spree.

Divide the teens into teams and assign them vehicles. Give each group a list of things they need to do in a limited amount of time. Each Silly Stunt will have points attached to it. Some stunts should have more points for each person doing it. The driver becomes the verifier that the stunt was accomplished.

Set a return time which they must arrive no sooner than 10 minutes before, nor 10 minutes later than, in order to earn points. Have refreshments waiting when they return. Groups will return over that 20-minute time span and will have a blast telling the other teens what they did and the strange reactions people had watching them do their stunts.

Include stunts they should do as a group, stunts individuals in the group can do, stunts they are to try to get other people to do, and stunts that get additional points for each person doing them.

Some stunts could include: having everyone kiss a statue; go to a hamburger place and ask for one french fry for each member of your team; have everyone get on a fire truck; see how many people you can get in a police car; have everyone join arm in arm and walk from one end of a mall to another; have each girl kiss a dog; have someone lay in a coffin; get a policeman to twirl a baton for you; get a paper shopping bag from a store and have five strangers sign it for you; tell a joke to four different strangers; get a band aid from a stranger; get three strangers to sing "Row, Row, Row Your Boat"; and whatever other crazy things you can think of.

2. Polaroid™ Party.

A Polaroid™ Party is similar to the Super Silly Stunt Spree. It uses the same time rule and some of the same stunts. The difference is, the team must capture the stunts on film.

Each group is given a Polaroid™ camera, one or two boxes of film and a list of things to get pictures of for points. The more people they get in the picture, the more points they get.

Be sure the camera works. Also be sure you have the right type of film for the lighting conditions under which your groups will work. Make sure someone knows how to operate the camera.

You may want to hang a piece of poster board for each team to display their pictures on when they return. Post those pictures around the church for a week or two. Use the pictures to promote the activity the next time you do it.

3. Sno-Lympics.

This is a great activity if you are in an area where there is snow and hills. Either meet at one central location or proceed directly to the area you will use for your competition. It would be best if you were the only ones at the area you plan to use.

Start with a general fun time of sledding while you wait for everyone to arrive. When everyone is present start specific events in which the teens can compete.

Some events to use include:

- *The Snow Ball Putt* – have categories for distance, accuracy, and size.

- *The Long Distance Sled Ride* – have individual and group competition.

- *Speed Sledding* – best times over a course for individuals and groups.

- *Tobogganing* – have categories for distance, fastest and slowest.

- *Tubing* – categories for fastest and furthest.

- *Creative Sledding* – individual and groups.

- *Snow Sculpturing* – individual and groups.

This is a good activity to close with hot cocoa, a devotional and an awards presentation.

4. Grubby O-Lympics.

This activity can be done inside or outside. It doesn't make much difference if you do this outside on a gloomy day because part of the fun is getting grubby.

Divide your group into teams which compete against each other, throughout the day, in a series of unusual events.

Some events which work well:

- *The Shot Put* – each team member tries to throw a variety of items the furthest. Items to use: Hershey Kisses, Plastic Bowling Pins, or Marshmallows.

- *Crawling Race* – the whole team crawls out and each member retrieves one item, thrown in the shot put. They can only use their mouth to retrieve the item. Choose a couple of team members to stay on the line and hold bags for the items to be placed in. Make each item worth different points.

- *Chain Relay* – each team lines up single file. The first person runs down and goes completely around a marker three times. They return, take the next person by the hand and run down and around the marker three times again and return for another person. They repeat this process till they have the entire team with them. If the chain breaks they must go back to the line, re-form the chain, and run that lap again.

- *Fill the Bucket Relay* – the goal is to fill a container at the other end of the line with water. Each team forms a single line with a small container at one end and a large container filled with water at the other end. With cups, bucker brigade style, each team relays water down the line, without skipping anyone, and tries to fill their container with water. The faster they go, the wetter they get.

5. *The Great Video and Game Challenge.*

This is similar to the Video Game-a-Thon. Divide the group into teams. Each teen tries to earn individual points which go toward a team total for the evening.

Use a combination of elimination and high score video games. Elimination games are those where two players play against each other. Use rounds for elimination. Each round will have half as many players in it, as they are eliminated. The finalists compete for a first place trophy. Some games like checkers, Ping-Pong, table hockey, and fooseball can be used for elimination.

High score games are those where the players try to get the highest score. Be sure all players get to play at the same level for the same amount of times. Darts and archery can also be used for high score games.

Use some table games like monopoly. Set a time limit for the game. If you have a lot of teens who want to play monopoly, have a few games going at the same time. The highest scorer from all the games gets the first-place trophy.

Make sure you have a couple of refreshment breaks, besides having some refreshments out all the time. Close with a devotional and award time.

6. *Gym Night.*

For a Gym Night you obviously need a gym. Break your group into two or four teams and have them pick captains. Use a variety of team games throughout the night. It helps to have some background music playing during relay games. Marching band music works great.

Start with games which involve everyone at first, then move to relay games, then games where representatives (usually the captains of each team) are chosen to compete. This gears you down to the conclusion of the event, where everyone is seated and ready for the devotional, which is followed by refreshments and fellowship time.

7. *Tire Night.*

This is similar to a Gym Night except all the activities are done with tires. This can be done inside or outside. Make sure you have a good quantity of the same size tires.

8. *Wild Goose Chase.*

This activity must be conducted in a town with some shopping places. It takes a lot of planning but is well worth it.

The object is to be the first team to arrive at a final destination and catch a goose. Refreshments and the closing program are conducted at that final location.

To find the final location, each team is given a starting clue. That first clue will lead them to a place where a person with the second clue is waiting. Each team is sent out in different directions and gather their clues in a different order.

The way they identify the person with the next clue is to walk up to someone at that location and say, "Goosey, Goosey Gander," to which the person with the clue will respond, "Where shall I wander?" If the wrong person is asked, they will most likely respond in a different way. When the right person is found and responds properly, the group tells the person their group number and is given their next clue.

The adult driver is given an extra copy of all of the clues, sealed and in order, with the answers. If the group cannot figure out a clue, they may ask the driver to open a clue and give them the answer. When they arrive at the final destination time is added on for each clue they open.

The first group to reach the final destination and catch the goose, without hurting it, is the winner. You can usually borrow a goose from an area farmer. It is usually best to have the goose staked to an area with a long rope so he can run around. Sometimes the goose will chase the teens, honking and trying to bite them, adding to the fun.

I have done this with as few as 12 teens to as many as 1,000 teens and every time the teens had a great time. We did this in one city and couldn't find a goose, so we got a white duck. (Ducks are less aggressive than geese anyway.) The duck got loose and everyone was running all over trying to catch it. Be sure to reward your goose or duck after the activity.

Others Activities

1. Adult Mystery Dinner.

This is a fun activity the teens put on for the adults. The teens prepare a mystery meal and a series of skits for the adults. Warn the adults in advance that this will be an unusual meal.

Prepare a mystery menu in advance. The menu should list all food items and utensils in code names. Salad could be called "Hope's Favorite Food." Ice cream could be called "Bob's Best." A fork could be called a "Facilitator." A knife could be called an "English essential."

The meal will be served in three courses: 1. appetizer, 2. main meal, and 3. dessert. The adults place a 1, 2, or 3, next to each item on the menu, indicating what course they want served. Some people may end up with ice cream and a knife..., etc.

Some people may end up with ice cream and a knife for their appetizer. Someone else may get soup and a fork for dessert. It all depends on the number they choose. A few people may have to eat some courses with their hands. Have plenty of napkins ready.

2. Ice Cream Parlor.

This is a nice activity the teens may put on as a family night at church or for an adult group. You could have a fifties or sixties theme. The teens decorate the room and set up some card tables with tableclothes and centerpieces corresponding to the theme. This could even be used during a missions conference with a missionary theme.

Some teens serve as waiters and waitresses and others dish up the ice cream. Offer cones, sundaes and sodas. The teens could provide skits, music or film as part of the evening. The activity could be conducted at no cost or as a fund-raiser.

3. Drama.

The teens work together on a dramatic presentation and present it for one segment of the church or for the church as a whole.

4. Concert.

The teens can either put on a concert using their own talent or they could put on a concert series bringing in other Christian musicians. This is conducted for the adults, children, the community or the church as a whole.

5. Talent Night.

This could be a talent competition among the teens. This works very well as a youth rally which encourages adults and children to attend.

Teens compete in the areas of instrumentation, vocal music, preaching, storytelling, puppets, and special presentations. Judging can be conducted by a panel of adult judges.

This could also be done as a church-wide talent night with the teens serving as the judges and the adults and children participating in the competition.

6. Film Festival.

The teens would arrange for a film or series of films to be shown for the church and/or the community and would plan a refreshment time afterwards.

7. Neighborhood Clean-Up or Help Day.

The teens would get together in groups and set out to clean up a road or part of a town. It is best to co-ordinate this with the town. Let the newspapers and local television station know what you plan to do.

For a Help Day teens can help local senior citizens with yardwork or housework at no cost. Many seniors cannot afford to pay for someone to do all of the work they need done. This is a great service opportunity for the teens. Put posters around town and at the local senior centers letting the seniors know they can call to get on a list of projects to be done that day.

8. *Street Meetings.*

This is an evangelistic opportunity where you take your teen group out on the street or to a park or beach for evangelism. You can conduct a program with singing, stories, testimonies, and a brief Gospel message. Teens can use their talents to draw a crowd. Everyone can help pass out flyers in advance. Some can do one-on-one witnessing. Reward your teens afterwards by doing something special.

There are many creative activities in which to involve youth that teach biblical principles, minister, and give opportunities to evangelize, and provide times of fun and Christian fellowship. I hope you will use these recommendations as well as others you may think of to disciple youth and involve them in the local church.

APPENDIX THREE

APPENDIX THREE
Starting Your Youth Ministry
Scheduling Your First Six Months to One Year

The following steps are a brief outline to help you revise your current youth ministry or help you start a new one. See the corresponding chapters in this book and the steps in the *Developing a Dynamic Youth Ministry* resource packet for in-depth planning aids and more details.

1. *Read the Book.*

Make sure you completely read and understand this book.

Have you read the book and do you understand it?

_____

2. *Enlist Your Leadership Team.*

Prayerfully select your youth workers.

Who will be your first team members?

_____   _____

_____   _____

_____   _____

3. *Begin Your Leadership Team Meetings.*

Start with your first monthly planning meeting. Make *general* plans for the next six months and *specific* plans for the next three months. Include Sunday School, clubs, team or youth meetings, activities and anything else for teens. Make plans for each item.

Then hold weekly Leadership Team Meetings.

When and where will your first monthly Leadership Team Planning Meeting be?

_____

When and where will you hold your weekly Leadership Team Meetings?

_____

4. *Plan a Destination Unknown (DU).*

This will be your first *Our Activity.* Let this serve as the kick-off for your new youth ministry.

Don't tell the teens where they are going or what they are going to do. Meet at the church. Divide into groups and send them off in cars to see who can find the destination first. Assign a teen captain for each car. Give the captain a set of directions to follow. Don't include road names or distinctive landmarks. Have them drive around in circles to confuse them. Plan a 20-30 minute drive. The last place should have a sign, "This Is Your Final Destination."

Give the driver a sealed envelope with the final destination and phone number inside. Don't tell the teens the driver has this. Have them open this only if they have not arrived at the final destination by a particular time. If they open the envelope and are more than 15 minutes from the final destination they should stop and call.

Have a good supply of pizza or some other kind of refreshments on hand when they arrive. Set some food aside for the latecomers. Play background music and allow time for fellowship until everyone arrives.

Have a brief devotional on setting a direction and having a goal. Explain what the new youth ministry will be like. Explain each facet of the youth ministry, what it is and what it entails. Introduce your team members and other workers who will be involved. Get a discussion going. Let them know they can get involved.

Date and Time for the DU

_____

Your Final Destination

_____

Drivers

_____   _____

_____   _____

_____   _____

5. *Begin Your New Weekly Youth Meeting.*

This can be Youth Sunday School or whichever of the planning options you selected.

When and where will your first Youth Meeting be held? _____

Who will lead the meeting?

_____

What will be taught?

_____

6. *Begin Weekly Teen Visitation.*

First this will be conducted by your leadership team members. Later, after you start your Teen Leadership Meetings, you will want to choose some teens who will serve as small group coordinators. They should be trained to visit, then take others along whom they will train.

It is a good idea to have people sign up in advance for teen visitation so each person coming will have a partner and someone to go to see.

When will your first Teen Visitation be held?

_____

Who will be your first visitation teams?

_____ and _____
_____ and _____
_____ and _____

7. *Hold a Second Our Activity.*

Plan a second *Our Activity*. Make this a real active, fun time. See the appendix on youth activities, for ideas.

What will the activity be?

_____

When and where will this be held?

_____

8. *Hold Your First Weekly Teen Leadership Meeting.*

Let the teens and parents know this is an in-depth study group for teens interested in learning to be leaders for Christ. Enlist some specific teens to attend.

Explain the teen leadership concept. Show them how to use the devotional notebook.

After the meeting, enlist small group coordinators and other teen leaders from those who attended.

When and where will you have your first Teen Leadership Meeting?

_____

What teens will you enlist to attend?

_____   _____

_____   _____

9. *Hold an Outreach Activity.*

Remind your teens this is an evangelistic activity. Choose a fun activity which you can do effectively.

What activity will you use?

_____

When and where will this be held?

_____

Who will bring the evangelistic devotional?

_____

10. *Hold a Low-Keyed Our Activity.*

Alternating an *Our* Activity with *Outreach* and *Others* Activities is a good idea. You can plan some real high-keyed *Our* Activities or some simple low-keyed activities. Be sure to alternate these. This Our Activity may be roller-skating, a hike or a low-keyed game night at someone's home.

What activity will you do?

_____

When and where will it take place?

_____

11. *Hold an Others Activity.*

Plan an activity where your teens do something for someone else. For starters, perhaps you could have your teens put on an activity for the children in the church. You may want to do a Gym Night or Field Day type of activity.

What activity will you do?

_____

When and where will it take place?

_____

12. *Begin Your Christian Service Program.*

Launch your Christian Service Program in your Teen Leadership Meetings. Your small group co-ordinators are already involved in Christian service. Provide some opportunities for Christian service for your other teens, either in your youth ministry or in other areas of the church. Start using Christian Service Forms.

Perhaps your teens would be interested in forming outreach teams for their Christian service. A puppet team, music group or drama team are all good outreach teams which can involve a number of people in Christian Service.

Who will coordinate your Christian Service Program?

_____

What opportunities for Christian service can you offer your teens?

_____   _____

_____   _____

_____   _____

When will you start your Christian Service Program?

_____

ORDER FORM

Quant.	Item #	Product Name	Price per Item	Total	Info. only (No charge)
	425T	*Becoming a Dynamic Youth Leader* textbooks	9.95		☐
	425	*Dynamic Youth Ministry* resource packet	79.95		☐
	407Y	*TEAM Mate Teen Planner* Youth Version (with free Leader's Guide) 1-25 copies, $2.00 ea. 26 or more, $1.49 ea.			☐
	425C	*Relationships: Living in a World Full of People* youth curriculum packet	29.95		☐
	425D	*Dynamic Devotions for Teens* 52-week book of daily devotions	9.95		☐

Shipping		
up to $3.00: **$1.00** $3.01 to $20.00: **$2.50** over $20.00: **$5.50** *Outside USA:* Add **$1.00** to above charges	**TOTAL ORDER**	
	Shipping (see chart)	
	Amount Enclosed	

Method of Payment:
☐ Bill Church (established accounts *only*)
☐ Check/M.O. Enclosed ☐ VISA ☐ MasterCard

Credit Card Account # ☐☐☐☐☐☐☐☐☐☐☐☐☐☐☐☐

Cardholder Signature _____ Exp. Date _____

NOTICE CONCERNING PRICES
The prices shown here reflect the prices at the time this text was printed. Since our resources are printed in bulk and placed in inventory, and prices are subject to change over time, the current prices may differ from what is listed here. Please confirm the prices at the time you order.

Check One:

☐ Pastor ☐ Youth Pastor ☐ C.E. Director ☐ Layperson ☐ S.S. Teacher

Name _____ Church _____

Address _____ City _____

State _____ Zip _____ Phone _____

Payment must accompany order unless your church has an established account with Church Growth Institute.

Please allow 2-3 weeks for delivery.

Send order to:

Church Growth Institute
Providing Practical Tools for Growth
P.O. Box 4404, Lynchburg, VA 24502